LET
Freedom
RING

LET Freedom RING

The Moral Foundations of a Free Society

STEVEN HORNE

LIBERTY HILL PUBLISHING

Liberty Hill Publishing
2301 Lucien Way #415
Maitland, FL 32751
407.339.4217
www.libertyhillpublishing.com

Library of Congress Control Number: 2021923642

Paperback ISBN-13: 978-1-6628-3709-8
Ebook ISBN-13: 978-1-6628-3710-4

Introduction

I wrote this book because I love liberty. I value my right to think my own thoughts, believe as I wish, and chose my own path in life. I don't like being told what to think or what to believe, let alone what to do with my personal life. I understand that there need to be restraints in life and that being free means I'm responsible for the consequences of my choices. But as long as I'm not trespassing on the rights of others, I want to be free to govern my own life.

Long ago, I recognized that if I want anything in life, I must give what I wish to receive; this is according to a universal law of cause and effect. It is known as the law of karma in Eastern philosophy and as the law of the harvest in Western thinking. It is articulated brilliantly by the American philosopher Ralph Waldo Emerson in his essay on *Compensation*, which I quote several times in this manuscript.

My approach to freedom is based on my belief in this law. I understand that the amount of freedom I ultimately enjoy is dependent on the amount of freedom I allow for others. If the law of the harvest is real, and we do reap what we sow, then the more I seek to restrict the right of others to think, believe, and choose, the more my own right to do so will be restricted.

The tyrants want freedom for themselves but want to be able to control others. Ultimately, they are not free. They are dependent on those they seek to control, who often reach the point where they rebel.

Tolerance is essential to a free society. Tolerance is a quality that allows us to peaceably disagree. It's expressed well in the phrase, "I may not like what you say, but I'll die to defend your right to say it." The right to disagree is essential to a free society because out of non-violent discussions, and even debates over issues, new ideas can arise that harmonize the apparently opposing beliefs.

For example, I'm an herbalist. I seldom use modern medicine; I mostly rely on diet, exercise, and other good lifestyle habits to maintain my health. When I do get sick, I usually treat myself with herbs and supplements. I teach people about what I know, but I would never try to force anyone to avoid modern medicine or rely on the remedies which I use. I'm not happy, however, when people who disagree with me wish to take away my right to care for my body as I see fit through government.

Likewise, I'm in an interesting position as far as my religious beliefs are concerned. I consider myself a disciple of Jesus Christ, but I don't belong to any Christian denomination. I never debate with people about religious doctrines. I enjoy listening to people with differing beliefs, even non-Christian ones, and try to glean useful ideas from everyone. I value our freedom to believe as we chose in America, and certainly do not wish to see that right diminished in any way by government interference.

The bottom line is that I'm comfortable with the fact that we disagree. As people try different things, we can observe and evaluate what works and what doesn't. When compliance with any idea is voluntary, I trust that the best ideas tend to rise to the top over time.

None of this holds true for political ideas, however. That's because politics is not about voluntary compliance or peaceful disagreement. Politics is about seeking to force one's ideas on everyone else, using government as a tool. That's why politics is a field that attracts tyrants and unless we understand the violent nature of government and restrain it with our moral beliefs, it rapidly gets out of control and destroys freedom.

Just like I have friends who belong to many different religions, I also have friends on both sides of the political spectrum. Many of my herbalist friends lean to the left. Most of the people who do business with me lean to the right. I have long tried to walk a middle ground, having an instinctive dislike for contention, but the deep, political divide in this nation is making it hard to find any middle ground.

Unless we can reunite around an understanding of the moral basis for liberty, I think our freedom is in danger of being lost. Once it is lost, freedom is seldom regained without bloodshed, something I genuinely hope we can avoid.

What I wish I could get everyone to understand is that government is violence; it is the use of force to try to compel obedience. When people wish to achieve their objectives through government, they advocate that their ideas should be forced on the world through violence. The danger lies in their success. If they do succeed in forcing their ideas on the world, the power they have created will cause them to reap the loss of their own liberties.

If the moral principles on which liberty rests were understood and practiced by a large enough percentage of the population (and I don't even think this has to be a majority), I think everyone, regardless of age, sexual orientation, race, religion, or economic status, would be better off.

I was raised to believe the Founding Fathers of America were inspired by God; I also believe God had a hand in forming this nation. These men were brave enough to advance these principles and stand in opposition to the greatest military and naval power in the world at that time. They put their trust in their Creator and succeeded with His help.

Just like most of my readers, I'm not rich, powerful, or famous. Yet, I believe I can make a difference and so can you. I firmly trust that ordinary people, armed with correct principles and acting with faith in God, have more power than the people who possess riches, political power, or large platforms on which to voice their opinions.

If you disagree with me, I'm OK with that, but I wish to close this introduction by paraphrasing an idea I got from my father—the philosophies of the world are simply profound but the truth is profoundly simple. I value that which is simple and plain. I find that it is the power-hungry who love complexity and hate common sense. Making problems overly complex and claiming that ordinary people are powerless to solve these problems is one of the primary, power-grabbing tools used by politicians. I do not believe in, or like, this elitist mentality.

You have more power than you realize, starting with the fact that you have an internal "truth detector" in the form of a conscience. The more you use it, the keener it becomes. Those who seek to wield power will always try to convince you not to heed your own instincts and inner wisdom; to conform; to go along with the crowd. Trust yourself. Think for yourself. Exercising your freedom to do so is essential to retaining it, just like exercising your muscles keeps them strong.

If, as I assert, the law of the harvest is a universal principle, then the more you are able to allow freedom for others, even in your personal life, the more you will expand your own freedom. Be humble, be tolerant, and trust in God, who "has chosen the foolish things of the world to confound the wise" and "the weak things of the world to confound the things which are mighty."[1]

May God bless you to uphold the banner of liberty in these challenging times.

Steven Horne
(August 2021)

---

[1] 1 Corinthians 1:27 (KJV)

TABLE OF CONTENTS

CHAPTER ONE

POLITICAL POWER

G overnment is dangerous; so is fire. This doesn't mean both aren't useful; it just means the potential danger in both needs to be understood and they both need to be handled properly to be useful.

Guns are dangerous too. Whether you favor private ownership of guns or you don't, you recognize this fact. Used properly, a gun can defend someone from harm or provide food for a family. Used improperly, guns can aid thieves in committing robbery or become an instrument of murder.

What is surprising is how many people don't realize that guns are the reason why government is dangerous. Governments use guns (and even more powerful and dangerous weapons) to impose their authority over people. There's a famous quote about this from the leader of the communist revolution in China, Mao Zedong, "Political power grows out of the barrel of a gun."[2]

No one knows for sure how many millions of people died as Mao implemented his political power, but various estimates range between 30 and 45 million people. Millions were also deprived of their freedom by being sent to Soviet-style gulags.

It's not just Mao either. If we look at all the various despots who arose in the twentieth century in Germany, Russia, and elsewhere, it has been estimated more than 100 million people died at the hands of

---

[2] "Problems of War and Strategy" (November 6, 1938), Selected Works, Vol. II, p. 224, as referenced at https://www.marxists.org/reference/archive/mao/works/red-book/quotes.htm

their own political leaders, which is more people than those who died in all the wars of that century.

That's why I find it ironic many people fail to see the danger in giving more and more power to the government. Perhaps it's because they confuse government with leadership. They think that government policies are put in place by voluntary co-operation, not weapons and violence.

A leader inspires people to join a cause and contribute their efforts to achieving it. While people in government can offer leadership, the government itself isn't based on leadership. It is based on the use of deadly force; it's based on guns. If you break one of the government's laws, you won't get a friendly person coming to you and *asking* you to *please* comply with it for the good of society. What you will get is an armed officer who will *demand* your compliance and pull a gun or other weapon on you if you refuse to comply.

Clearly, how we chose to handle this power is important. It can be used to protect us, but it can also be used to destroy us. The Founding Fathers of America understood this and with this understanding, they entered into one of the greatest social experiments ever conducted. They tried to find a way to harness the deadly force of government so that it would serve, rather than subjugate, the people.

How Would You Handle Political Power?

Many of us are "armchair" politicians. We talk about what government should or shouldn't be doing with a great deal of conviction. Some of us even write letters to government officials or perhaps even join a protest. It's easy to decide what other people should do when there aren't any real consequences to your ideas. But suppose you were given real political power; how would you handle it?

To answer that question, I'd like you to join me in two little thought experiments. A thought experiment is a logical argument or mental model that one creates by visualizing an imaginary or hypothetical scenario. This is a perfectly valid way to experiment with ideas. One of the most brilliant scientists the world has ever known, Albert Einstein, did thought experiments, which helped change our entire understanding of the nature of the universe.

If it's good enough for physics, it's certainly a good enough approach for politics. For thought experiment number one, I'd like you to imagine that you've been given the ultimate in political power. I'd like you to visualize yourself as the dictator of the entire world.

As the world dictator, you have all the military and police powers of the world at your command. These loyal followers are ready to enforce whatever laws you deem necessary for the good of the world. You can now fine, imprison, or even kill anyone who resists you and your laws. There is no one above you who can or will punish you for what you decide.

I'm suggesting you do this because it's one thing to express how things "ought" to be. It's quite another thing to actually use force to compel people to obey you. So, if you had this power, what would you do with it?

Perhaps you're an environmentalist. You believe mankind is adversely affecting the climate, threatening all life on the planet. So, in this thought experiment, you now have the power to force whatever changes you want to stop people from polluting and destroying the world. What are you going to force people to do? If people with different views oppose you, are you going to fine them, imprison them, or perhaps execute them?

Perhaps you are a compassionate person who sees the poor and underprivileged people of the world and wants to make sure that everyone on the planet has food, shelter, clothing, and health care. You can now tax anyone and everyone and use this money you collect to fund your world-wide welfare programs. If someone opposes you and refuses to pay their taxes, you can have them arrested and confiscate their property to fund your effort. Furthermore, if they resist your tax officers, you can have them killed. How do you feel about that?

Maybe you're concerned about violence and public safety. You decide that only people in the government who are under your orders should have guns. You feel this will reduce crime and make the world a more peaceful place. So, you send men and women armed with guns to confiscate the guns of those who own them. If they refuse to surrender their weapons, there will be bloodshed because if they resist your efforts with their own guns, they will be killed, as will some of your officers. Do you feel comfortable with this?

Maybe you're a very religious person. You feel that society is rampant with immoral behavior—drugs, pornography, alcohol, sexual perversion, and abortion. You want to make all of these things illegal. Are you willing to have drug addicts and alcoholics arrested or possibly even killed if they oppose your laws? Do you want to put homosexuals in jail or execute them (something which happens in some middle-eastern countries)? Do you want to imprison women and medical personnel who participate in abortions? Whatever you decide, it's very possible that people will die while you're enforcing your laws. Is that right? Is it moral?

Maybe you think that believing in God is delusional and want to ban religion outright. Many communist countries held to this idea and millions of religious people were slaughtered or imprisoned or labeled as mentally ill and forced into hospitals for the insane. Are you ready to do that? Are you ready to end people's lives just because they believe that there is a power higher than you, which requires their obedience to that power instead of yours?

We could go on and on, citing numerous topics of hot debate in our modern political climate. I'm not arguing for or against these policies at this point, even though I do have my positions on them. I'm merely trying to point out one thing—government uses guns and violence to impose its will. Therefore, whatever you ask government to do, you are saying violence is the way these ends should be achieved.

Maybe you sincerely believe that the end result of enforcing your policies will make the world a better place and, therefore, violence is justified. That's what Hitler, Stalin, Mao, and many other dictators have thought. Maybe you don't. I just want you to think about it.

If you're a Christian, you should really think about it. The last temptation Satan offered to Jesus was to have full control of all the kingdoms of the earth. He offered him the opportunity to make the world a better place by taking over every government on the planet. All Jesus had to do was worship Satan. Jesus turned him down and took another path to change the world. Would you?

How You Do You Exercise Power?

The first thought experiment is a set-up for the second. We're going to move from the global scale to the personal scale. Governing the world, after all, is a big task. How about governing just your family, friends, and neighbors? What would you do if you were given dictatorial power over your immediate circle of influence?

Imagine you've been given complete authority to compel anyone within that circle to do anything at the point of a gun. If your wife, your children, your extended family members, your friends, and your neighbors don't do whatever you order them to do, you have the full authority to force them to obey at gun point. If they resist, you have full authority to shoot them if necessary. No authority is higher than you, so no one can punish you if you compel their obedience.

What are your rules going to be now? Will you threaten to kill one of your neighbors if he doesn't pay you the taxes you want to feed other neighbors who are poorer? Will you threaten to kill your child or your friend for littering or using too much gas in their cars? If one of your neighbors is drinking alcohol or smoking pot, will you strap on your gun and order them to stop?

The most important question is this: Will the laws you force on your family, friends, and neighbors be the same laws you would force upon the entire planet? You might think, yes, but I doubt you really would. When it comes to our immediate relationships, most of us don't see violence as the best solution. There are some very abusive people who do, but I'm guessing that most of us wouldn't want to threaten our spouse, children, or neighbors with a gun and force them under threat of imprisonment or death to do whatever we thought was right. There's really no love or friendship in that, is there?

Both of these thought experiments are asking you the same question: "What is the moral use of force?" I'm asking you, when do you think someone is morally justified in using violence (knives, guns, or worse) to threaten people and compel their obedience? This is a moral question and a critical one for our times.

Morals are the standards we use to determine right from wrong. Our morals dictate how we treat other people, both those close to us and those who are strangers. Many, if not most, people have double standards when it comes to morals. They have one set of moral standards for those they perceive are "on their side" and another set of moral standards for those on the "other side."

People are more likely to be lenient and forgiving to someone who is one of the "us," while more willing to use force with one they perceive as part of the "them." The "us" versus "them" can be political, religious, national, racial, or cultural, but the truth is that most people given dictatorial powers would utilize this double standard. They would force their policies on the world at large but be far more tolerant, and even indulgent, with those they consider to be family or friends.

After all, that's pretty much what communist leaders, fascists, and dictators have all done. It's even true in America, as members of Congress have passed laws to enforce on everyone except themselves, and high-ranking officials often get away with crimes for which you or I would be severely punished.

You don't need to be a political dictator to have this kind of double standard in your moral reasoning. Think of all the parents who tell their children either literally, or by the discrepancy between their words and their actions, "Do as I say, not as I do!"

Sound Moral Reasoning

I wouldn't want absolute political power. I've never sought to be a dictator, even in my own family or as the boss of my own business. I like freedom, both for myself and for others. That doesn't mean I don't believe there is a moral justification for force. Some amount of government is necessary. Whether you're a parent, a boss, or a political leader, there are occasions when force is morally justified.

I wrote this book to help people think about this question of force and morality, especially in the realm of government. However, I'm also asking you to consider how this applies to how you treat others close to you. What I am presenting isn't just a political philosophy; it's a philosophy that governs my interactions with family, friends, and business associates as well. For me, morality doesn't change with the number of people involved or the relationship I have with them.

Returning to politics, however, I have come to recognize that there is a clear line between political power that protects and enhances freedom and political power that advances tyranny. America is the only country we know of that has at least tried to embrace the principles I'll be discussing, although as I will point out, America has never fully implemented them.

Still, the American ideal is unique in that we are the only country in the world founded on the idea that government was supposed to *serve,* rather than *rule,* the people. In the words of Abraham Lincoln in the famous Gettysburg address, it is a "government of the people, by the people, for the people."[3] Lincoln's phrase may have been adapted from

---

[3] Abraham Lincoln, "The Gettysburg Address", November 19, 1863, http://www.abra-hamlincolnonline.org/lincoln/speeches/gettysburg.htm

an earlier declaration by Daniel Webster, who said that the American government was "the people's government, made for the people, made by the people, and answerable to the people."[4]

This ideal, put forth by the men known as the Founding Fathers of America, has resulted in the great American experiment. Lincoln saw the struggle of the Civil War as one that would determine whether this form of government and the moral ideals that fuel it could long endure. Today, we again find ourselves in the same struggle. Will the ideals of the Founding Fathers will continue or be lost?

What is unfortunate is that the understanding of the moral principles that laid the framework for the American experiment is largely already lost. We need to rekindle these principles in the hearts and minds of the people. We need to help people understand why these principles are vital, not only to our national survival but to the future of the entire world. My prayer is that my voice will help reawaken people to the great ideal of liberty and its moral foundations.

You may not agree with all of my ideas, but that's the beauty of freedom. You are free to disagree, and I fully support your right to do so. If we lose the right to disagree, liberty will be destroyed. So, with that in mind, let's begin.

---

[4] Daniel Webster, "Daniel Webster's speech in the United States Senate on the slavery compromise." March 7, 1850, https://www.goodreads.com/work/quotes/6040848-webster-and-hayne-s-speeches-in-the-united-states-senate-on-mr-foot-s

CHAPTER TWO

LIBERTY IS IN DANGER

On July 4, 1986, I returned to America after spending three weeks touring communist China. I had been visiting China as a member of an herb company's corporate team. They were launching a line of traditional Chinese herb formulas. We had toured traditional hospitals and pharmacies, visited a farm where herbs were grown, and met with many manufacturers of traditional Chinese medicines. We had also visited the Great Wall, saw the Terra Cotta warriors, and walked through the Stone Forest. We even had dinner with the governor of Tibet. It was a once-in-a-lifetime experience; eye-opening and often scary, but certainly enlightening.

Nevertheless, here I was, back on American soil on the same day celebrating the signing of our Declaration of Independence. I was relieved to say the least, since I had actually feared for my life on several occasions when I was in China, mostly from taxicab and bus drivers. So, after passing through customs in San Francisco, I understood the feeling people have when they want to kiss the ground. I was back in a prosperous country where I felt safe and relatively free.

The extreme poverty and third-world conditions I witnessed in China were distressing. I had seen Chinese families living in 10x10 structures that were identical to the storage lockers Americans use to store their excess belongings. When in China, I couldn't call home and almost all of the letters and postcards I sent home arrived after I got back. I remember when our party needed to make a long-distance call to the next city we would be visiting. You called the operator, gave the number, and she called you back when she was able to make the connection. It took about two hours to make that connection.

The airports in major Chinese cities were like run-down Greyhound bus stations in America. You had to go to the airline office the day before and show your ticket. They had a piece of paper with the image of the plane and its seats. They wrote your name down on the correct seat by hand to reserve it. The closest I'd seen to a plane leaving on time was just two hours late. Most of the time, our flights were about four hours late.

Everywhere we went, a member of the Communist party accompanied us, making sure nothing said to us was "politically incorrect." Our translators often spoke with the party representative before translating the conversation. I assume they were getting approval as to what they could and couldn't say.

One of the stops we made was in Lhasa, Tibet. As I mentioned before, we had dinner with the Chinese governor. That experience, more than any other, burned the fear of government power into my soul.

For those of you who are not familiar with the history of China and Tibet, you need to know that Chinese troops marched into the Tibetan capital of Lhasa in September of 1951. Since that time, one fifth of the population of Tibet (about 1.2 million people) have died as a result of China's policies. Over 6,000 monasteries, temples, and other cultural and historic buildings have been destroyed. According to a petition submitted to China by the 10th Panchen Laman in 1962, "more than 97 percent of monasteries and nunneries were destroyed and the number of monks and nuns living in the monasteries was reduced by 93 percent."[5]

The signs of Tibet's occupation had been evident. Soldiers with machine guns were stationed on bridges and at other strategic locations.

---

[5] "Revisiting the 'Cultural Revolution' in Tibet," https://tibetmuseum.org/revisiting-the-cultural-revolution-in-tibet/

The tension was obvious when I was there and a little more than a year later, it broke into protests and riots that lasted two years. But there I was, shaking hands and having a pleasant dinner with the political leader in charge of the Communist occupation.

Awakening to a Truth About Politics

So, what scared me? It was simply this — he didn't fit the stereotype I had in my mind of evil dictators. He was friendly and pleasant. In fact, he seemed very much like the few American politicians I'd had the privilege of meeting. I think he sincerely believed that what he was doing was right and was for the benefit of the Tibetan people.

The phrase "power corrupts" seemed applicable. I recognized that ordinary people, when given political power, can easily be convinced to use it in ways that destroy innocent people's lives in order to advance some agenda or ideology.

I was very familiar with the constitutional idea of division of powers. I understood why the Founding Fathers had worked so hard to separate pollical power both horizontally — through the three branches of government: the legislative, executive, and judicial — and vertically, by the idea of state, county, and local governments. Giving any one individual, no matter how well-intentioned he or she is, too much power is inherently dangerous.

As James Madison said in Federalist Paper #51:

> If men were angels, no government would be necessary. If angels were to govern men, neither external nor internal controls on government would be necessary. In framing a government which is to be administered by men over men, the great difficulty lies in this: you must first enable the government to control

the governed; and in the next place oblige it to control itself.[6]

But I realized, at the time, government isn't very good at controlling itself. People in power routinely believe that they are the enlightened ones, the people who know what's best for everyone else. They sincerely believe they know what's best for you and me and that having that power, they can and should use it to control us, the "unenlightened."

Over the course of my life, I've witnessed firsthand how the federal government continually exceeds its authority under the Constitution. More and more power concentrates in the federal government, and more and more power gravitate toward the executive branch of the federal government. Thus, the government violates both the vertical and horizontal separation of power.

Why does this happen? Because it's more efficient, of course. It's a cumbersome process to try to get many different people to agree on anything. If you believe you know what's best, you don't want to have to convince people you're right; you just want more power to force your will on others.

My trip to China awakened me to a great truth. The greatest check against tyranny isn't the Constitution; it's the moral beliefs of the American people. It's not the government's job to preserve our rights and our liberty — it's the job of "we the people."

On that July day in 1986, I realized that our liberties were safe as long as the majority of Americans believed in the moral principles upon which our rights are based. And, at the time, I thought Americans would never stop believing in freedom of religion, freedom of speech, freedom of the press, the right to keep and bear arms, and free enterprise. That's what made me feel safe in America. I was back in a country where I believed the majority of people held fast to these basic principles.

---

[6] Federalist No. 51 (1788-02-06)–Federalist Papers (1787–1788)

There is a New Civil War in America

My sense of security in America started to be broken nearly 25 years later, in 2011, when I started experimenting with social media as a tool for growing my business. I had stopped watching the TV news many years earlier, as I felt it focused too much on the negative side of life. I wanted to concentrate my energy on trying to do good in the world, not worrying about all the bad things that were going on.

As I read posts by many young people on a website called Tumblr, I became aware that an increasing number of young Americans no longer believe in many of the aforementioned ideas. Schools and colleges were filling them with ideas that went contrary to the ideals I understood America was founded on. One of these ideas is that a person is justified in using violence against people who disagree with you if their views constitute "hate speech." I also realized they were also being taught that America was an evil country, and that free enterprise was actually exploitive.

I've had a lot of opportunities to travel internationally since that trip to China in 1986. In addition to another trip I made to China in 2006, I've traveled across Canada, visited the UK, Malaysia, Jamaica, and I've even been to Russia twice. My wife is from Ukraine and the stories she tells of corruption and poverty in that country, both during and after the Soviet occupation, are disturbing, to say the least. The fact is that people who haven't traveled extensively have no idea how well off we are in the United States, both in terms of freedom and in economic opportunity.

My primary concern is that we've lost the understanding of the moral laws that keep us free. In fact, we've already lost a great deal of our freedom, especially in two areas—economics and due process of law. Unfortunately, most people can't see this because they've never understood the principles behind these ideas, nor understood what the Constitution was supposed to guarantee. It's also why I don't blame these young people for being upset at the "system," since in many ways it has failed them. They are unable to be prosperous in the same way their grandparents were, as inflation has outstripped the buying power of their earnings.

I worry about this because I don't think the people I spoke to in Communist China in 1986 had any idea how little freedom they enjoyed. I remember a conversation I had with one of our translators while riding in a taxi without the Communist party person present. She told me how free China was after the Communists had overthrown the Chinese emperor.

She told me about their equivalent to our "4th of July." It's called National Day of the People's Republic of China and celebrates the day that Chairman Ma Zedong formally declared the establishment of the People's Republic of China. That day was the first public parade of the People's Liberation Army. As she explained, they have festivities, sports and cultural events, fireworks and concerts, just like we do. And all of this is to celebrate their "liberation."

As the famous German author Johann Wolfgang von Goethe said, "None are more hopelessly enslaved than those who falsely believe they are free."[7] I was friends for eight years with an ex-CIA agent. One of the things he told me was that black slaves were discouraged from learning to read. Why? He said that slaveholders knew that if blacks were educated, they would realize they were slaves and rise up and rebel. Brainwashing people to think that they are free when they are simply conforming to the majority opinion doesn't mean they actually are free.

The Constitution of the United States has a preamble, which states the intent of the document and part of the intent of "We the People" is to "secure the blessings of liberty to ourselves and our posterity." But the Constitution doesn't define what liberty means. It is our other founding document, The Declaration of Independence, which does that and that is what we will look at in the next chapter. Without

---

[7] Johann Wolfgang von Goeth, "Geothe's Opinions on the World, Mankind, Literature, Science, and Art, 1853, p. 3, http://libertytree.ca/quotes/Johann.Wolfgang.von. Goethe.Quote.282D

the insights found in the Declaration, we can't understand what the Constitution was seeking to secure, which is why the next chapter is devoted to defining liberty.

CHAPTER THREE

DEFINING LIBERTY

A desire to be free exists deep within the human soul. Children start expressing this around age two, as they start saying "no" to parental instructions. Teenagers express it when they rebel against family rules. Couples express it when they fight about their partner's demands for behavioral change. It expresses itself in the political landscape, as individuals and party affiliates fiercely disagree about social issues.

Our desire to be free is counterbalanced by our social nature. Children may say "no," but they also want parental love and attention. Teenagers seek more freedom but still want family help and support. Partners in marriage want to make their own decisions, but also want their partner's love and approval. The tension between these two desires means there are two forces at work forming society. One is the desire for freedom while the other is the desire to belong.

As Americans, ideas like "do your own thing" and "have it your way" are imbedded in our national consciousness, but most of us would never take this to the extremes that Satanist Aleister Crowley did when he wrote, "Do as thou wilt shall be the whole of the law."[8] If the only law was, "Do whatever you want," then nobody would be safe or secure. None of us want to be murdered, have our property stolen or

---

[8] "Do What Thou Wilt," http://tim.maroney.org/CrowleyIntro/Do_What_Thou_Wilt.html

vandalized, or to be enslaved by another stronger person who claims he is just exercising his freedom to "do his own thing."

That's why true liberty is founded in morality. There has to be a limit to freedom. There has to be a place where our ability to have our own way ends so that others around us can be free too.

The ideal of freedom that ignited the American revolution and the constitutional republic that grew out of it was one that was rooted in the value and dignity of the individual. It was Thomas Jefferson who eloquently penned this idea into the Declaration of Independence.

> We hold these truths to be self-evident, that all men are created equal, that they are endowed by their Creator with certain unalienable Rights, that among these are Life, Liberty and the pursuit of Happiness. That to secure these rights, Governments are instituted among Men, deriving their just powers from the consent of the governed.

I believe these words were inspired by God because they were a radical change in the thought processes that had governed people for thousands of years, in spite of the fact that the signers were claiming these truths were "self-evident." They were so radical, in fact, that the Founding Fathers were not able to fully implement them.

Many of them recognized that slavery was incompatible with this ideal, but it would take a future generation, and a bloody war, to free the slaves. It would take many more generations, and the turmoil of the 1960s in which I grew up, to start dismantling laws that supported discrimination. Native Americans weren't treated as equals either; neither were women. Nevertheless, these words laid forth an ideal toward which America has been striving and toward which progress has been made.

However, even if we've never fully implemented this ideal, it still lays forth the basis for freedom. Each person is endowed with *unalienable rights*.

What are Unalienable Rights?

The word unalienable means you cannot be made an alien to your something—in other words, it cannot be separated from you. It means you possess rights by the very fact that you are alive. They are as much a part of your nature as your eyes, ears, hands, and mouth.

The Declaration of Liberty states that these rights are unalienable because they were not given to you by man. They were given to you by the Creator, by God Himself. This idea that rights come from God has largely been forsaken in modern American discourse. First, because there is a growing trend toward atheism and secondly, because we tend to talk about constitutional rather than unalienable rights.

Unfortunately, talking about constitutional rights gives the idea that the government gives us these rights, which means the rights come from other men, not from God. If the rights are granted by men, then men also have the power to take them away. That is also true if there is no God, no ultimate moral authority. If God does not exist, then unalienable rights are merely an idea proposed by some people that other people can chose to ignore because it interferes with them "doing their own thing."

The idea of human rights is not a political issue; it is a moral issue. Believing your rights are God-given and unalienable is essential to a free society for two reasons. First, if those in political power believe there is an authority higher than themselves, who will hold them morally accountable if they trespass on other's rights, it will help to restrain their actions. More importantly, if the people believe that these rights are given them by God, and not by some earthly mortal authority, they will defend their rights and seek to prevent other people, including those acting on behalf of government, from taking them away.

There is a second reason why it's important to recognize that your rights come from God and not man—you can't believe that other people are going to automatically respect them. No rational person could believe that. After all, there are people who try to violate your unalienable rights from time to time and, many times, they actually succeed.

What the concept of unalienable rights means is that no one (including those who are in authority in government) has the *moral* right to deprive you of them. If they trespass against your rights, they are morally in the wrong, and since they are morally in the wrong, you morally have the right to resist their efforts. In fact, it means you have the moral right (and perhaps even the moral obligation) to use violence to protect yourself or others against said violation.

Understanding Our Unalienable Rights

The Declaration of Independence lists our basic rights when it declares that *among* our rights are the rights to life, liberty, and the pursuit of happiness. I emphasize the word among to indicate that the list given here was never meant to be exhaustive. However, I would also suggest that all our other rights are extensions of these basic rights. Let me elaborate on each of these three basic rights and their moral foundations.

THE RIGHT TO LIFE

Mankind cannot create life. We can't even create a single, living cell. Therefore, life is something that we cannot give, which also suggests it is something we should have reverence toward.

The idea that human life is sacred is rooted in the biblical idea that God created human beings, male and female, in His own image. God breathed the breath of life into mankind and made us living souls. The moral right of life is also defended in one of the ten commandments, "You shall not murder." Exodus 20:13 (NKJV)

We all have an instinctive, God-given desire to preserve their own lives. In fact, most of us would consider murder as the most serious of all criminal acts because our desire to live is unalienable to our souls. Even those seeking to take the lives of others will act to preserve their own lives at the same time. A person has to be extremely traumatized, deeply psychologically wounded, and/or mentally ill to lose the desire to live, illustrating the unalienable nature of the right to life.

There are extensions to this unalienable right. Someone doesn't have to kill me to diminish my life. Anything that damages my body is a trespass against my life, which is why we also consider assault to be a crime. If someone knocks out my teeth, pokes out my eye, tortures me, or poisons me and destroys my health, we can also see that as a trespass against our right to life.

The right to live is the most basic and overarching of all rights. Without it, the other two basic rights can't be exercised. No one can enjoy liberty or pursue their happiness after they are murdered, and their ability to exercise liberty and pursue their desires is diminished when they are injured. That's why every sane person seeks a life free from bodily harm inflicted by other people.

THE RIGHT TO LIBERTY

The biblical story also indicates that God gave mankind free will, granting them the power to choose to defy Him if they so desired. Free will would not be possible if we had no ability to choose between right and wrong. Free will was a dangerous gift because choosing evil means that mankind has the capacity to cause a great deal of pain and suffering in this world. But God still offered this gift to mankind.

The idea of free will isn't just our capacity to choose between good and evil, however. In its most fundamental nature, it is the capacity to create. When God, the Creator, formed man in His image, He granted him the capacity to create and, to me, that is what liberty is really all about.

Liberty gives us the freedom to choose what, how, and when we will create. It allows us to express the life God has granted us. We are able to pour the energy of our lives into whatever constructive (good) or destructive (evil) activities we desire.

The creative capacity of human beings is something you do not see in the animal kingdom. Animals create things of course. Spiders make webs, birds make nests, and gophers dig tunnels. But these creative acts are distinctive to each animal. Spiders don't make nests, gophers don't spin webs, and birds don't dig tunnels. As human beings, we can do any of these things. It is our creativity and self-consciousness (the ability to reflect on ourselves) that make us unique among the other forms of life around us.

When society respects people's liberty, it is amazing what human beings are capable of discovering, inventing, building, transforming, and otherwise creating. Think of all the amazing benefits we enjoy in a free society because of the creative efforts others make in art, science, industry, and business.

Most of our so-called "constitutional rights" are merely extensions of our right to liberty. We can believe or disbelieve what we want. We can write or say what we want. We can travel where we want. We can protect our own lives and property against criminals by being armed. We can choose those with whom we will associate and form voluntary and mutually beneficial agreements with them.

Other than restricting our freedom by forbidding us to trespass on the rights of others, the idea that God wants us to be free is deeply rooted in the Judeo-Christian ideas that shaped the Founders' thinking. In his discussion of the Ten Commandments, Dennis Prager, the Jewish founder of Prager U, points out how the first of the Ten Commandments demonstrates God's desire for mankind's freedom. It begins, "I am the Lord your God, who brought you...out of the house of bondage" (Exod. 20:2, NKJV).

Mr. Prager notes that God could have said, "I am the Lord, your God, who created the Universe..." but God chooses to emphasize His role in setting them free. It suggests that God is opposed to slavery. In fact, the story of Moses leading the children of Israel out of bondage in Egypt was an inspiring ideal in the American Revolution; so much so that Benjamin Franklin suggested an image of Moses parting the Red Sea for the national seal.[9]

The biblical narrative also suggests that God granted us the ability to become co-creators with Him in forming the conditions of this world. However, as I will discuss later, this also means that we will be held accountable for what we chose to create.

THE RIGHT TO PROPERTY

The philosophers of the enlightenment that brought about the American concept of government, such as John Locke, spoke of our three basic rights as "life, liberty, and property." Thomas Jefferson used the term, "the pursuit of happiness" in place of property.[10] Apparently, he wanted to convey that there is more to life than just acquiring property, a concept to which today's consumer-driven society needs to awakened.[11]

Still, one aspect of the pursuit of happiness is the acquisition of property. That's because property is essential to preserving both life and liberty. We require food, clothing, and shelter in order to sustain our lives. We may also require other types of property to exercise our creative liberty and achieve our individual goals. Builders need tools,

---

[9] "Benjamin Franklin's Great Seal Design," https://www.greatseal.com/committees/firstcomm/reverse.html

[10] "Creating the Declaration of Independence: Pursuit of Happiness," https://www.loc.gov/exhibits/creating-the-united-states/interactives/declaration-of-independence/pursuit/index.html

[11] "The Unalienable Right to Pursue Happiness in the Declaration," https://www.loc.gov/exhibits/creating-the-united-states/interactives/declaration-of-independence/pursuit/index.html

musicians need instruments, farmers need seeds and farm implements and photographers need cameras.

Thus, property is also an extension of the rights of life and liberty. As I exercise the creative power of liberty, I create things. Because I have put part of myself (my life energy, time, and liberty) into my creations, they are mine. Ownership is the final right of control; that which I own I am free to use or dispose of as I see fit.

I can use my property for my own purposes; sell or trade it for something else I want; give it away or even throw it away. If I own something, no one else has the right to determine what I do with it. I have no moral right to the property of another, as expressed in the commandments, "You shalt not steal," and "You shalt no covet." (Exod. 20:15,17 NKJV)

Possessions are not necessarily property. If a man snatches a woman's purse on the street, the purse is not his property, even though he is in possession of it. If I acquire something through theft, deceit, or fraud, then what I am in possession of is not my property, either.

But there is a further distinction we need to make between possession and property, one our society often fails to make. I did not create the natural resources found on this earth. I did not create the air, water, land, plants, or animals. I can take possession of these resources, but it is my added labor that makes them mine.

It is therefore fundamentally immoral to deprive other human beings access to the resources God created to sustain human life. For instance, we should not be locking up unused land and labeling it private property, because it's a fundamental fact that every person needs land to occupy in order to live (something I discuss in chapter 14). Freedom does not mean we can deny others land to live on, air to breathe, water to drink, and access to the other resources needed to create the food, clothing, and shelter they need to survive. Such actions are blatant violations of other people's right to life.

THE RIGHT TO PURSUE HAPPINESS

The above discussion of how the pursuit of possessions or property can be used to justify harm to others is why the phrase "the pursuit of happiness" is an important ideal. Jefferson appears to have based this phrase on the idea of happiness expressed in ancient Greek and Roman texts, where happiness is linked to morality and virtue.[12]

Aristotle argued that happiness was not equivalent to wealth, honor, or pleasure. In the Nicomachean Ethics, he wrote, "the happy man lives well and does well; for we have practically defined happiness as a sort of good life and good action."[13] Jefferson admired the Roman philosopher Epicuris and summarized his ideas in a letter to a friend, stating that happiness is the aim of life, but that virtue was the foundation of happiness. He also stated that utility (the benefits our lives produced for our fellow man) was the test of virtue.

Clearly, Americans have lost sight of what it really means to pursue happiness. Genuine happiness is not found in the things most people are chasing, such as wealth, fame, or power. It is found in morality, virtue, and goodness. Therefore, our unalienable right to property does not mean we have a right to pursue all the material wealth we can get, especially if it is done at the expense of others. Rather, it is our right to pursue the highest good to allow our souls to achieve that which is just, right, and true.

RIGHTS ARE NOT PRIVILEGES

In today's world, people use the word rights very loosely. Mostly, they use it in reference to "group rights." They speak of gay rights, black rights, female rights, and so forth. Group rights are not rights. Anything which other people have to grant you is not an unalienable right; it is a privilege.

---

[12] J. David Gowdy, "Thomas Jefferson and the Pursuit of Virtue," http://www.liberty1.org/TJVirtue.pdf

[13] Carol V. Hamilton, "Why did Jefferson change 'property' to the 'pursuit of happiness,'" https://historynewsnetwork.org/article/46460

By definition, the *unalienable* rights we have just discussed must be both individual and universal at the same time. They are inherently part of each *individual* person, and they are also universally part of *every* individual person. Your unalienable rights either belong to everyone or they belong to no one.

They don't belong to us because we are part of a specific race, gender, religion, or nationally. From a spiritual perspective, if our unalienable rights were only available to us because we are of the "right" race, sex, religion, or nationality, then God would be a respecter of persons. Unlike human beings, God is "no respecter of persons," (Acts 10:34 KJV) so what He grants to each of us, He grants to all of us.

I firmly believe that God wants every person on this earth to enjoy the rights He gave them. I also believe that He will hold us accountable in the hereafter for our trespasses against the rights of others if we do not repent of those trespasses. Although the Founding Fathers had many different religious beliefs, they recognized that a belief that God would hold men accountable for how they treated each other was an essential moral foundation for America. To the extent that we have lost that belief, our rights are under attack because crime and lawlessness will increase when people do not believe they will ultimately be held accountable by a just God.

CHAPTER FOUR

CRIME IS TRESPASS

O nce we understand the unalienable rights to life, liberty, and property, and that these rights are God-given gifts to each individual, we have established the understanding of crime. A crime is a trespass against the unalienable rights of another individual. In fact, this was the original, constitutional definition of crime.

In a course I took on American common law, from George Gordon's School of Common Law during the 1980s, he claimed that the original definition of crime in the United States was "a deliberate and willful trespass against the life, liberty or property of another, in which there is a demonstrable loss of life, liberty or property." I have searched for the origins of this definition and have not been able to find it. However, I think it is the most valid definition of crime I've ever encountered.

Here's why crime should be defined in this way. First, a crime must involve a victim. To call something a crime where there is no victim is an abuse of power. There are many victimless "crimes" in modern society and when a crime has no victim, it really means it's only a crime because some human being decided it should be a crime. Without this concept, the idea of crime loses its moral foundation.

Next, this definition of crime defines who a victim is. To be a victim means that some aspect of your life, liberty, or property has been lost and that loss must be demonstrable. Demonstrable means that I have to be able to objectively demonstrate what was lost. The injury can't be subjective. I can't claim someone is guilty of a crime because they hurt my feelings. If that's a crime, every single one of us is a criminal many times over because all of us hurt other people's feelings, both intentionally and unintentionally. It may not be polite or kind to say hurtful things to each other, but it's not a criminal activity.

Third, to establish a crime was committed, it must be demonstrated that the trespass was "deliberate and willful." This means the person had intent to trespass against my rights. Something that accidently or unintentionally caused a loss is not a crime. A small child who picks up a loaded gun, not recognizing its dangerous nature, and kills someone with it is not a criminal.

One can seek recompense for harm caused by negligence or neglect, but this action falls under civil law, not criminal law. Civil law is law that is designed to keep the peace by arbitrating disagreements between citizens where no crime has been committed.

Crime versus Sin

There is a strong relationship between the idea of crime and the idea of sin; however, all sins are not crimes. Sin has been defined as "falling short" or "missing the mark." The idea of sin suggests that we fall short of God's perfection. So, not everything that one might consider a sin fits the definition of a crime.

Doing things that cause harm to our own lives, health, liberties, and properties could be considered sins, but they aren't crimes, and we shouldn't treat them as such. For example, people damage their health by overeating and becoming obese; they lose their liberty when they use drugs and become addicted; and they can gamble away their life savings, but none of these things are crimes because there is no victim. If so, the person would be both the criminal and the victim, as there was no perpetrator other than the person him/herself. This person is falling short of her or his own potential, but he or she is not deliberately and willfully causing harm to others.

This is an important distinction to make because many well-intentioned people often want to use government to enforce moral standards on other people. Prohibition was one of these attempts. When an amendment to the Constitution was passed to allow the government to forbid the sale of alcohol, the production and sale of alcohol went underground and turned otherwise law-abiding citizens into "criminals."

A similar thing has happened with the prohibition of marijuana. One might argue that the drug pusher is trying to sell products that damage people's health and, therefore, trespass against their health, especially if they're pushing their drugs on children, but the drug user is not a criminal and shouldn't be punished. Instead, they should be helped. The drug pusher, on the other hand, could be punished if they are "deliberately and willfully" selling something they know is harmful to others.

The same thing could be said for laws that prohibit sexual acts between consenting adults. One may see these acts as sins, but where there is no victim, there is no crime. On the other hand, rape, child molestation, and sexual relations with minors can all be considered crimes because there is a victim, who either did not give consent or was in a position where their immaturity prohibits them from giving proper consent.

Likewise, if I get drunk or stoned in my own home, I may be sinning but I'm not acting in a criminal manner. On the other hand, if I get drunk and beat my wife and children, I have committed a crime. If I get stoned, drive a car, and get into an accident where others are injured or killed, that *could* be considered a crime if it can be proven that I did so with deliberate intention. But, even if it is determined that I didn't deliberately and willfully seek to harm others, I can be held liable for damages under civil law.

Having clarified that, let's re-examine each of the rights we listed earlier and see how each right is related to this definition of crime.

Crimes Against Life

Murder is an obvious trespass against the right to life, but as we previously indicated, anything that causes damage or injury to a person's body is also a trespass against life because their capacity to experience life fully has been diminished. Thus, assaulting another person and causing demonstrable, physical injury to his or her body, such as causing him or her to go blind in one eye, is also a crime.

By this definition, deliberately doing something to cause the person to become sick would also be a crime. So, if I'm deliberately selling something I know to be harmful to human health, I am committing a crime. I am also committing a crime if I deliberately poison people's water, food or air and make them sick. This is an important to understand because it relates to environmental issues and business practices.

If I manufacture and promote a product I know to be defective and potentially harmful to other people's lives, that's a crime, especially if I have hidden the harmful effects of the product and made false claims it was safe. If I'm deliberately dumping toxic waste into the environment and making other people sick, that's also a crime.

When there is no proof that the action was deliberate and willful, it does not mean that we can't use civil law against businesses that are polluting or producing harmful products. It just means the actions are considered negligent, not deliberate or willful.

Crimes Against Liberty

To attempt to control the constructive choices of another person by violence or threats of violence is also a crime. This means that enslaving another person/people, kidnapping them, or forcing them to engage in activities they have not voluntarily and willingly consented to would be a crime against someone's liberty.

In addition to the obvious crime of slavery, a crime for which America has paid dearly, crimes against liberty include kidnap, rape, sexually molesting children, and forcing another person/people to do something under threat of violent punishment if they do not comply. This would include forcing people into involuntary associations (such as marriage or a church) and contracts (such as business deals).

It would also be a crime to violently prevent people from exercising their rights of conscience, such as peacefully worshipping God in their own way or expressing their personal opinions or beliefs. Censorship or trying to silence another person through any violent means is therefore a crime.

Crimes Against Property

As previously explained, when people engage in honest work and acquire property or possessions as a result of that honest work, they have a right to decide how that property is to be used. So, any act which deliberately and willfully damages, destroys, or takes their property is a crime. Taking someone's property is the crime we call theft or stealing. The crime of vandalism is damaging or destroying someone's property. Arson is another crime.

One can also steal someone's property through extortion or forgery. One can steal through engaging in dishonest transactions, where one deliberately misrepresents a product or service and takes your money but fails to deliver what was promised. Crimes done by deception, however, are usually processed under civil rather than criminal law.

Modern society also recognizes something called intellectual property. The ability of a person who invents something new to take out a patent so they can enjoy the profits from the sale of their invention is one example. Artists, writers, movie-makers, and so forth are protected by copyright laws, which allow them to receive money from the benefit of their labor. There are similar protections in place now for software developers.

The right of property is a sticky issue in some respects. Society must have some standards for what defines property, how property is exchanged or transferred, and other rules that make commerce, industry, and even the right of property possible. We'll address some of these later. For now, I think it's easy to see that robbery, arson, vandalism, and other similar trespasses against property qualify as crimes.

Common Law and the Golden Rule

The idea of crime we have just referenced is sometimes referred to as the *common law*. The common law is the law that is common to just about everyone. People in general recognize that these things are crimes when they are the victim of them. We have a sense of moral indignation when someone trespasses against our lives, liberties, or properties. We also recognize it's wrong when it's done to someone we care about. We acknowledge this when we say, "That's just not right!"

The idea of common law is rooted in what is known as the Golden Rule. The Golden Rule is expressed in the New Testament as follows.

> Therefore all things whatsoever ye would that men should do to you, do ye even so to them: for this is the law and the prophets. (Mat. 7:12, KJV)

> And as ye would that men should do to you, do ye also to them likewise. (Luke 6:31, KJV)

The Golden Rule isn't just Christian, however. It is found in most of the world's religions in one form or another. It is found in Buddhism: "Hurt not others in ways that you yourself would find hurtful" (Udana-Varga 5:18). Confucius taught it thusly, "What I do not wish men to do to me, I also wish not to do to men" (Analects 15:23) and "Try your best to treat others as you would wish to be treated yourself, and you will find that this is the shortest way to benevolence" (Mencius VII.A.4).

Jesus Himself was referring to a passage in the Old Testament when He cited the Golden Rule. "...thou shalt love thy neighbor as thyself" (Lev. 19:18). Native Americans saw the principle as extending to our relationship with all living things, not just other human beings: "All things are our relatives; what we do to everything, we do to ourselves. All is really One" (Black Elk).[14]

As the examples above illustrate, the Golden Rule can be stated in the positive or in the negative. The positive expression is "treat other people the way you would like them to treat you," or "do unto others as you would have others do unto you." The negative expression is, "don't treat other people in a way you wouldn't want them to treat you" or "don't do anything to someone else that you would not want them to do to you." It's this negative application of the Golden Rule that allows our understanding of what constitutes a crime. The Founding Fathers recognized this as the natural law, "the law of nature and of nature's God."

The nearly universal nature of the Golden Rule is the result of something God has also planted in the heart of every human being—a conscience. Our conscience is the still, small voice found inside of us that tells us what is right and what is wrong. Conscience is associated with compassion, which suggests the idea of "common passion" or "common feelings." Because we feel hurt, angry, and sad when someone trespasses against our unalienable rights, our compassion should tell us that other people have similar feelings when we trespass against their rights.

The youngest children scream out in pain when someone hurts them. They fear threats to their lives and health. They express grief and anger when something they created is destroyed or taken from them, or when they are forced to comply with things they don't want to do. This shows how unalienable this concept of rights is to our human nature.

Understanding this universal common law and the nature of crime sets the stage for understanding justice. Just like the idea of common law is based in the Golden Rule and conscience, the concept of justice is based on the law of the harvest and our desire for satisfaction when

---

[14] All of the above are referenced at http://www.religioustolerance.org/reciproc2.htm

we feel wronged. This is important, because government should be just, that is have its moral foundations rooted in justice.

CHAPTER FIVE

JUSTICE AND THE LAW OF THE HARVEST

J ust as the Golden Rule is prevalent in many different spiritual philosophies around the world, so is the principle of justice. It is known as the law of the harvest in the New Testament, the principle of "an eye for an eye" in the Old Testament, and the law of karma in Eastern religions. This principle is even found in physics, which tells us that for every action there is an equal and opposite reaction.

Justice is associated with the law of cause and effect, which I'll refer to as the law of the harvest throughout this book. It's expressed in the phrase, "As you sow, so shall you reap," which is adapted from Gal. 6:7 (NKJV), "Be not deceived, God is not mocked; for whatever a man sows, that he will also reap."

Any farmer or gardener knows that to grow the crop you want, you have to plant the right seeds. The crop is pre-determined in the nature of the seeds. In like manner, our actions reap consequences in harmony with their nature. In other words, the choices I make are the seeds I plant and the results I experience in my life are the crop I reap.

Freedom gives me the right to choose the action, but it does not give me the liberty of choosing the reaction. I can't plant corn seeds and expect to reap a crop of wheat. The reaction (effect) is built into the nature of the action (choice).

Like any law of nature, the law of the harvest operates whether we believe in it or not. That's why the Scripture stresses, "God is not mocked." We all recognize that the laws of nature can't be violated. I can choose to step off a cliff, but I cannot choose to fall up. If I say, "I don't believe in gravity," that won't stop gravity from operating on me.

The law of the harvest works in this same way. If the law of the harvest is a universal rule, then the Golden Rule isn't just a nice sentiment. It's a rule I ignore at my own peril. It isn't just that I *should* treat others the way I would like them to treat me; it's warning me that the life I will reap for myself will be *dependent* on the nature of how I chose to treat others.

Ralph Waldo Emerson went to great lengths to explain the inescapable nature of the law of the harvest in his famous essay *Compensation,* found in *Essays, First Series.* In it, he claims:

> Crime and punishment grow out of one stem. Punishment is a fruit that unsuspected ripens within the flower of the pleasure which concealed it. Cause and effect, means and ends, seed and fruit, cannot be severed; for the effect already blooms in the cause, the end preexists in the means, the fruit in the seed.[15]

Emerson further declares, "You cannot do wrong without suffering wrong."[16] He also insists, "...because of the dual constitution of things, in labor as in life there can be no cheating. The thief steals from himself. The swindler swindles himself."[17] If you have not read *Compensation,* I highly encourage you to read it and if you have read it, re-read it.

---

[15] Ralph Waldo Emerson, Essays – First Series (Kindle Edition, 2012), p 72

[16] *Ibid.*

[17] *Ibid.* p 80

Freedom, Accountability and Responsibility

The law of cause and effect links freedom to the principles of responsibility and accountability. My freedom only extends to my *choices* (cause); it does not extend to the *consequences* (results) of those choices. The consequence is the natural outgrowth of my choice and is *automatic* in the nature of how the universe functions.

The law of the harvest impresses upon us the inescapable *responsibility* that goes with freedom. While I am capable of using my own agency to trespass against the unalienable rights of another person, the law of the harvest says that I am *responsible* for the trespass and I can, and ultimately will, be held *accountable* for it.

There are many people who do not believe this principle. They believe that they can "cheat" and obtain "something for nothing." But the law of cause and effect clearly tells us that for every action there will be an equal, and opposite, reaction. Thus, as Emerson says, you cannot do wrong without suffering wrong.

The punishment for doing wrong, Emerson assures us, is sure and swift:

> All infractions of love and equity in our social relations are speedily punished. They are punished by fear. Whilst I stand in simple relations to my fellowman, I have no displeasure in meeting him... But as soon as there is any departure from simplicity, and attempt at halfness, or good for me that is not good for him, my neighbor feels the wrong; he shrinks from me as far as I have shrunk from him; his eyes no longer seek mine; there is war between us; there is hate in him and fear in me.[18]

---

[18] *Ibid.* p 78

He elaborates on this, saying:

> Has a man gained anything who has received a hundred favors and rendered none? Has he gained by borrowing, through indolence or cunning, his neighbor's wares, or horses, or money? There arises on the deed the instant acknowledgment of benefit on the one part, and of debt on the other; that is, of superiority and inferiority.[19]

The Law of the Harvest and Justice

When I make a free and unrestrained choice, I am responsible for the outcome of that choice. If I chose to initiate violent action against another and trespass against another person's unalienable rights of life, liberty, or property, I have planted a seed. The person whose rights have been trespassed against is going to feel violated and angry with me. He will justly have cause to seek restitution and other honest, moral people will support him in that desire. Hence, I have opened myself up to violence being justly measured out to me.

To someone who doesn't believe in God, the big issue is not getting caught. That's why the Founding Fathers knew that the only foundation that would keep the government they created working was the moral integrity of the majority of the citizens. If you're one of the people who believes that there is no higher authority than man, and man-made government, I assure you that the law of the harvest is real and it will act on you.

Understanding the law of the harvest lead us to the understanding of justice, which is a practical operation of the law of the harvest. Under the common law, as long as every person in a society is respecting the unalienable rights of others, we have equity or equality in a society. Everyone gets treated the same by the law; thus, the law is common to all.

---

[19] *Ibid.* p 79

When a person violates the common law by committing a crime, they made a decision to not treat their neighbor as they would want to be treated. They have breached the equity of society by not seeing their neighbor as an equal. They have judged that their desires were more important than their neighbor's rights.

Under the common law, a trespass creates in-equality in society. This in-equity (which is shortened to create the word iniquity) must be corrected if all the members of society are to continue to be equal. That's where justice comes in.

Justice is a scale of social balance or equity between people. It is based in our sense of what is fair, which is tied to our conscience. It is also how we properly answer the question, "When are we morally justified in using force to deprive another person of life, liberty, and property?" The word justified in this sentence is the same as saying, "When is it just (or fair) to use force and violence?"

The answer is that we are morally justified in using force against those who have trespassed upon the rights of others in a society. The role of justice is to correct this inequity and restore the social balance, which is why justice is often depicted using an old-fashioned balance scale.

Casting our Moral Vote

The individual who violates the common law has cast his or her moral vote against one or more of the unalienable rights. In deciding the other person did not have the right to their life, liberty or property, they have basically decided that this right doesn't exist. Therefore, society is justified in trespassing against their right to their life, liberty, or property in an equal degree.

The criminal can be held *accountable* for the trespass because they are *responsible* for the consequences of their actions, which caused loss and suffering on the part of their victim. A moral society will therefore be justified in in forcing the criminal to correct the in-equity between them and the person or persons they trespassed against. If society allows for the trespass, then it encourages others to trespass as well, increasing crime in society and a breakdown in respect for the rights of others, and for the idea of law and order in society.

A similar thing happens when government uses excessive punishment. People who feel that the law is unfair or unjust also won't respect law and order, which ultimately threatens the peace of the entire society.

This is why only a society that offers "liberty and justice for _all_" can endure in peace. Any faction or minority in a society that is being denied their unalienable rights will not only _feel_ justified, they will _be_ justified in fighting against the iniquity that is being committed against them.

Chapter Six

Punishment versus Restitution

I n this chapter, I want to address one of the ways in which the American system of government fails to uphold the principles of common law and justice. I consider this the greatest moral failure in our society. There are a few other such problems in our society I'll address later, but this is the most serious and fundamental flaw in our government.

This flaw is that we think justice involves punishing people instead of compelling them to make restitution. This problem arises because the majority of people firmly believe that we teach people to be moral by rewarding them for being "good" and punishing them for being "bad." I assume that most people reading this were raised by parents who used rewards and punishments to discipline them, so it's natural for us to believe that this is the only way to make people be good. We believe this so deeply that we even see God as the rewarder and punisher of good and evil.

I hope to help you see justice in a different way by the end of this chapter. My understanding of these principles started out in my search to be a more effective parent. As a young father, I took a parenting class my last semester at the university. My oldest daughter was 10 months at the time.

In the class, I was introduced to the book *Children the Challenge* by Rudolph Driekers, which taught me that rewards and punishments are ineffective parenting tools because they create power struggles between parents and children. The power struggle destroys feelings of goodwill and cooperation between parents and children.

Driekers suggests that you want to win cooperation with children rather than try to force obedience. This is done through the use of natural and logical consequences, which are designed to help children learn to control themselves rather than being controlled by you.

The concepts presented in *Children the Challenge* made perfect sense to me, because I had already come to accept the idea of the law of the harvest, which says that what we chose to do in life has built-in consequences. So, I put these principles into action and discovered that they made parenting a very enjoyable and rewarding experience for me. To this day, I love working with children because I understand what motivates them and can rapidly get them cooperating with me.

So, what does all this have to do with government? Well, if rewards and punishments create problems and disharmony in a family, destroying the spirit of love and cooperation between parents and adults, then I would propose that they do the same thing in society. The attitude that we can reward (bribe) people into doing good and deter them from doing evil by threatening them with punishment is at the very foundation of just about everything government does.

In fact, some people seem to believe that if we apply enough force by passing enough laws, we will be able to control human behavior to the point that we will prevent anyone from ever doing anything wrong. This is simply not true. It's not true because in a society, just as in a family, the more force and coercion you apply the more you destroy the spirit of goodwill and voluntary cooperation that is the essence of healthy human relationships.

It is important to understand that human beings are by their nature social creatures. As explained in chapter two, our desire for freedom is balanced by our need to belong. When love and goodwill exist between people, they do not deliberately trespass against each other. If there is an accidental trespass or one born out of a temporary loss of goodwill, parties tend to seek reconciliation naturally, without the need of a third-party like government.

So how is this applicable to society at large? If we don't seek to bribe and punish people to make them good, what do we do to dispense justice? The answer is surprisingly simple. We apply the law of restitution, which is a human application of the law of the harvest.

The Law of Restitution

The Founding Fathers studied many governmental systems from history. The Greek and Roman republics, the reign of the judges in the Old Testament, old Anglo-Saxon law, and even the government of some Native American tribes. They borrowed many ideas from these places, but one idea they did not utilize was the idea of a restitution-based judicial system.

The goal is restitution is not punishment but rather compensation to the victim for his or her loss. It is aimed at restoring equity and can even be used to facilitate reconciliation between the victim and the trespasser.

In our state-mediated punishment system, people are typically fined or jailed for criminal activity. Occasionally they are even given the death penalty. The fines, however, are paid to the state, not the victim. If the trespasser is jailed, the victim is paying taxes which are used to keep the trespasser in prison.

Although we call this a justice system, it should really be called a judgement system, for it does nothing to restore equity. Nothing is done to compensate the victim for their loss, except perhaps fulfill a need for revenge.

Under a restitution-based legal system, justice requires that the victim be compensated, "eye for eye and tooth for tooth" for their loss.

This does not mean that a person who gouged out someone's eye is supposed to have their eye gouged out. It's about the fact that the victim who lost the eye or tooth through the deliberate and willful trespass of another is entitled to a just compensation from the trespasser.

It's not the state that has been wronged by the criminal actions of a trespasser, it's the victim(s) who have been wronged. Justice needs to be on behalf of the victim(s), not on behalf of the state. Justice really involves the balancing the scale of social equity.

Restitution in Theft

To give a practical example of this, let's look at how both the Old Testament and Anglo-Saxon common law systems handled stealing. In them, a robber was required to make payment to the person from which he stole. Depending on the situation, the thief would need to pay anywhere from two to seven times the value of what was stolen to the person they stole from.

To understand why the thief is required to do *more* than just return the stolen property requires a little explanation. Let's say that the theft stole a loaf of bread (as Jean Valjean does in the story *Les Misérables*). If the theft were required to restore only the loaf of bread he stole, he would only be returning what was never rightfully his. The thief has suffered no loss of his own property, so the scale of justice remains unbalanced.

But by having to compensate the victim with two loaves of bread, the theft has not only returned the property that was never his to begin with, he has also suffered a loss of his own property equal to the loss which he inflicted on his neighbor. Equity has been restored "eye for eye," since the thief has experienced the same loss he inflicted, no more and no less.

It's simple and logical. Plus, it's not based on the emotional desire for revenge. Justice isn't supposed to be based on emotion, but rather on the facts and the evidence. Emotionally, victims tend to want revenge, which really arises from the desire to see the trespasser suffer emotionally in the same way the victim is suffering emotionally. Restitution, on the other hand, is born out of the practical and logical need to restore equity between the parties.

This brings us to the reason why restitution could be higher, up to seven times the value of what was stolen. Why on earth would it be just to require someone to pay seven loaves of bread for having stolen one? This provision covers for the possibility that a rich man stole from a poor man, whose suffering and loss was greater, proportionally, than the rich man's. The rich man is required to compensate the poor man with more property, only so that he will feel a loss that is more comparable to the loss he inflicted on the poorer man.

For those familiar with the Old Testament, I suggest you review the principles of the Mosaic law to see the various ways it provided for compensation to victims of a crime. Skip the religious rituals and focus only on the penalties for crimes. It will give you a whole new understanding of what the phrase "an eye for an eye" means.

Negotiation to the Victim's Satisfaction

If you look at Old Testament law, you'll see it prescribing death for a lot of situations in which the death penalty seems overly harsh. However, after doing a little study, I found that Jewish people understood that the prescribed penalties were the maximum, allowable restitution. Victims did not have to seek, nor did judges have to grant, the maximum allowable restitution.

Under Old Testament law, five possible forms of restitution are prescribed: a public whipping, fines, imprisonment, banishment, and death.[20] Death is _required_ only for premeditated murder. A lesser "satisfaction" (meaning a lesser compensation to the victim) can be made for all other crimes, but it is the victim who must receive the satisfaction.

---

[20] For a more complete explanation of this legal system see: Cleon Skousen, The Majesty of God's Law (Riverton, UT: Ensign Publishing, 2010), "The Philosophy of Penology Under God's Law," pp 52-54.

It is likely that banishment would be used instead of the death penalty in most cases, other than murder, where the death penalty is prescribed. Being "cut off from among the people" (banished) from society isn't possible to enforce unless there's an implied, "Don't come back under penalty of death."

In all cases, where the death penalty was prescribed as a potential "satisfaction" for a victim, the injured parties and the witnesses upon which the verdict was rendered were required to initiate the execution. Since this was done by stoning, literally throwing rocks at someone until they were dead, the victims and witnesses had to "cast the first stone(s)."

In other words, the execution had to be undertaken by victims of the trespass and their witnesses. This fact alone could make it more likely that judges could have negotiated a lesser restitution to the victim.

For example, although many spouses feel murderously hurt and angry upon learning that their partners have cheated on them, most wouldn't actually want to kill their spouses. After the initial anger "cooled off," the injured spouse would probably just want to get on with their lives. So, they would likely settle for a lesser restitution—a share of the joint property and custody of the children, for instance.

But if the cheating spouse was also abusive and threatened their lives, they may also want the former spouse banished for their own safety. The "death penalty" aspect of this means that if they violate their "restraining order," their spouse has a right to use deadly force to stop them. That's what I believe the "death penalty" aspect of this law is really about. I again recommend you study and ponder the principles of Old Testament law more closely under this light.

Judges Under the Common Law

This leads to the third and final aspect of the common law system of the ancient Israelites and Anglo-Saxons. The judges who heard these disputes and resolved them were selected by the people through a democratic process, just as they are in America today.

Both the Israelites and the Anglo-Saxons organized themselves by family groups. The smallest group was ten families (or in modern times, we'd say households). These groups were also organized into larger groups of fifties, hundreds, and thousands. All of the judges over these groups were chosen in yearly elections.

Under this system, if you had a complaint against someone, you took it first to the leader of your group of ten families. They were required to try the case and make their decision. Appeal could be made to the higher judges if either party was dissatisfied with the judgment.

The judges were only consulted over disputes. They did not dispense rules. In fact, they only became rulers in the case of a national invasion where the judges automatically became the captains of the able-bodied men who could be mustered to defend the nation.

So, let's imagine we're living under such a system today. In fact, suppose you are one of these judges elected by the other nine households in your neighborhood. Your role is to hear disputes from the citizens and render judgment to compel restitution to the satisfaction of the injured party. Because these people are your neighbors and you are accountable to them because they can replace you, you would be motivated to encourage the parties to work out an amicable settlement, wouldn't you?

This means that these restitution-based common law systems were not just intended to simply be a way of meting out prescribed restitution. Instead, there would be some desire to arbitrate disputes in a way that aimed to restore peace and equity to the neighborhood.

Thus, the goal of the systems was to teach people to be accountable for how they treat each other according to the Golden Rule. Once I understood this, I realized why Jesus could say that loving God and loving your neighbor as yourself was the basis for *all* the law and the prophets. If the goal was simply punishment, then how could it help restore love between neighbors?

The American System of Common Law

American government has its roots in the idea of common law. This means that everyone is supposed to be free as long as they don't trespass against their neighbor or break the voluntary agreements they've made with others. This means leaders aren't supposed to be rulers; they are supposed to be servants of the people. Instead of ruling, government is supposed to exercise its power in three ways.

First, government is supposed to set up and maintain the framework or structure that helps create a level playing field for everyone so their rights can be protected. That's what the American Federal and State Constitutions do, along with the applicable laws and rules that govern how the system works. Right now, that's not working very well for reasons which I will attempt to elaborate on later.

Second, government is supposed to help protect us. Part of this should be providing a way for victims, whose rights have been trespassed against, to get help in finding restitution. Criminal law deals with those who trespass within society and military law maintains discipline for those who are supposed to protect us from outside threats. However, as I've already pointed out, our system is missing the restitution part of this process. Restitution is only meted out through civil law.

Third, when private citizens can't agree with each other and work out their differences, such as a divorce or a breakup of a business partnership, the government provides a system for arbitrating disputes. That's civil law. The reason for this arbitrating of disputes should be to restore peace and equity, although it often doesn't work that way.

These facts are what make our government a republic, meaning our government is a system of laws, not a ruler or group of rulers. It's very important to understand that America was not created as a democracy, but rather as a republic based on common law, as we'll discuss in the next chapter.

CHAPTER SEVEN

A REPUBLIC, NOT A DEMOCRACY

O ne of the greatest problems threatening our freedom is the idea that America is a democracy instead of a republic. Think of the Pledge of Allegiance, which states, "and to the republic for which it stands." It does not say, "and to the democracy for which it stands." Substituting democracy for republic when talking about the American system is a deliberate attempt to move people away from the true principles and ideals that founded America.

To understand the difference, we first need to understand that there are two, and only two, basic concepts of government. This is very different from the left versus right idea of government, with fascism on the far right and communism on the far left.

The real difference is between ruler's law and common law. Ruler's law is by far the most common form of government, and both fascism and communism are examples of it. The thought experiments, proposed in chapter one, were both exercises in ruler's law, where you, as the ruler, get to decide what the law will be.

The other, more rarely practiced, form of government is a common law republic. In a common law system, it is the law which rules the people, not the ruler. That's why it is also known as the "rule of law."

Ruler's law says, "He who rules makes the law." This means that the authority of the government is vested in a person or group of people.

The person or persons who rule decide what is right and wrong and use their power to seek to force obedience to these standards onto everyone else. So, under ruler's law, the people who run the government decide what is and what is not a crime. Under ruler's law, the idea of justice is to punish people who disobey the government authorities.

We readily recognize the danger of ruler's law when the authority to make the laws and enforce them upon others is vested in a single person, such as a monarch, emperor, or dictator. The term for this form of government is monarchy. The "archy" part of this word derives from the Latin *archia* and the Greek *arkhia,* which means rule, and from arkhos, which means ruler, commander, or chief.[21] *Mono* means one, which means there is one ruler or one source of government authority.

In any type of monarchy, the one ruler may decide at whim to use the power of government to trespass against the unalienable rights of those under his or her rule. The ruler may steal from his subjects, force them into slave labor, and even kill them and claim it is moral because he, the ruler, is the source of the law.

The fact that the king of England was trespassing against the rights of the people, rather than protecting them, was the reason the thirteen colonies rebelled. The Declaration of Independence primarily consists of a list of ways in which the colonists were being unfairly treated by England. These abuses of dictatorial power were forth as the justification for refusing to consent to the king's rule. (As a side note, most of these abuses of power have also become a part of our current government, showing how far we have strayed from the principles of freedom.)

However, ruler's law is not confined to governments in which there is a single leader. The power to determine the law can also be vested in a particular group of people. For instance, one can have a theocracy, where those who adhere to a particular religion are the rulers. Communism is

---

21 "-archy," https://www.etymonline.com/word/-archy and https://affixes.org/alpha/a/-archy.html

also a form of ruler's law. In this case, the rulers are a group of people who adhere to a common ideology (the Communist party).

Communism and theocracy are similar in many ways. They are both built on an ideology that is imposed upon society using government power. Both are oligarchies. The prefix *oligo* comes from the Greek *oligos*, which means few, scanty, or small.[22] In an oligarchy, a privileged few rules over the many.[23] Under both systems, those who have differing views are silenced, suppressed, and punished.

Under any system involving ruler's law, there is no equality or equity in society. Society is divided into two, unequal camps: the ruler or ruling class and the common people.

Democracy is a Form of Ruler's Law

What most Americans fail to recognize is that a democracy is also a form of ruler's law. In a democracy based on majority rule, the majority can impose their will on the minority. This again creates two classes of people: those in majority and those in the minority. That's why democracy has been called mob rule. Whoever can persuade the mob (a majority of the people) gets to make the rules, which are then imposed on the minority. That certainly creates inequity in a society.

The only way to avoid this is a democracy based on consensus, where everyone has to agree. That may be workable on a small scale, such as within a family, but I doubt we could ever get hundreds of millions of people to agree on much of anything. This is why John Adams said in a letter to John Taylor in 1814, "Democracy never lasts long. It soon wastes, exhausts and murders itself. There was never a democracy that did not commit suicide."[24] Benjamin Franklin was concerned that "When the people find that they can vote themselves money that

---

[22] https://www.etymonline.com/word/oligo-

[23] Merriam-Webister, https://www.merriam-webster.com/dictionary/oligarchy

[24] John Adams, "Letter to John Taylor," 1814, http://www.john-adams-heritage.com/quotes/

will herald the end of the republic."[25] There is also a quote widely attributed to Alexis de Tocqueville, author of *Democracy in America*, which says, "The American Republic will endure until the day Congress discovers that it can bribe the public with the public's money."[26]

The contention in American party politics stems from a belief in democracy, rather than a belief in the rule of law. The parties represent ideas that groups of people wish to force the rest of society to follow. So, we wind up fighting and arguing, primarily through the political parties, each of which is vying for the power to force the other half of our society to comply with their point of view. The result is a growing political division. If one side wins, the other side loses. Unhealed, such a division pushes us towards civil war—which is pretty much the "suicide" that John Adams warned about and, as I write this book, we seem very close to that reality.

This situation also leads to a bigger and bigger government with more and more control over our lives. Each party pushes for bigger government in its own way, whether it's military spending or spending on social programs. The argument isn't over whether government should have that power over our lives or not, but only who should get the money and the power.

No wonder politics stirs up such anger in people. Our love of liberty causes us to fear people with imposing views because we know they want to force us to conform to their rules. In all of this, we are missing the fundamental ideal as set forth in the Declaration of Independence, which is that we are all equal and have equal, unalienable rights.

The Consent of the Governed

A true republic is the other form of government, but it can only function and endure when the laws of the republic are moral. In a republic,

---

[25] http://libertytree.ca/quotes/Benjamin.Franklin.Quote.CC66

[26] https://due.com/blog/alexis-de-tocqueville-bribing-the-public-with-their-own-money/

the governing power lies with "we the people." But, contrary to pop-ular understanding, "we the people" does not mean the opinion of the majority. We the people are the *individual* people in this country, who are forming a government to protect and preserve our individual, unalienable, God-given rights.

Referring back to the Declaration of Independence, we read: "...to secure these rights, Governments are instituted among Men, deriving their *just* powers from the consent of the governed..." In other words, the purpose of the government is to secure the rights of *each person* living within the country, not the opinion of one group or another. When the government steps outside of this role of imposing equity or justice, the government is no longer just and according to the Declaration of Independence, the people have the right to alter or abolish it.

Remember that this passage says that government derives its "*just powers* from the consent of the governed." In contrast, govern-ment can derive *unjust powers* from the majority view or sway of the mob. When the majority decides to try to use the government to take away the unalienable rights of the minority, we cannot have a safe or peaceful society.

The word republic breaks down as "re-public," or having reference to the public. While communist countries can claim to be republics, as in the People's Republic of China or the Union of Soviet Socialist Republics (USSR), they are not republics in any real sense of the word because they do not protect the rights of individuals in their coun-tries. The unalienable rights of the public is not the source of the moral authority of government under communism. Instead, that system is based on the idea of collective (group) rights, which I earlier called privileges.

In a true republic, it is the common moral law understood by the public that is the basis of the government. Righteous people resist tyranny and government leaders really do depend on the "consent of the governed" to maintain their power. If enough people rise up in rebellion against government policies, politicians cannot maintain their power. To a certain extent, this idea also applies to all governments. They depend on the consent (or at least the general compliance of the governed) for a stable society.

The leaders of the Jews in the time of Jesus wanted Jesus arrested and killed because He spoke against their authority, but they "feared the people" (Mark 11:18, 12:12; Luke 20:19, 22:2). All unrighteous governments "fear the people" because if the people wake up to their immoral actions, they will turn against those who govern them. So, governments can only exist as long as a large percentage of the population "consents" to be governed.

Morality is Essential to Maintain Freedom

The Founders knew that the constitutional republic they had created could not survive if the majority of the people in America become immoral. They knew that the "mob rule" of democracy will cause the government to trespass on the rights of others, destroying the equity in the society. That's why John Adams said, "Our Constitution was made only for a moral and religious people. It is wholly inadequate to the government of any other."[27]

That quote points to the very issue that prompted me to write this book. Good government is based on the morality of the people. As people become increasingly immoral, government will increasingly violate people's unalienable rights. As the story goes, a lady asked Benjamin Franklin at the close of the Constitutional Convention of 1787, "What have we got, a republic or a monarchy?" He is said to have replied, "A republic, if you can keep it."[28]

If we return to the moral principles I'm discussing in this book, America would sow good seed and reap good results. Unfortunately, we

---

[27] John Adams Historical Society, "Quotes," http://www.john-adams-heritage.com/quotes/

[28] https://www.ourrepubliconline.com/Author/21

are on the verge of losing our republic by misapplying the principle of democracy and because of the increasing lack of moral understanding about the foundations of good government.

CHAPTER EIGHT

HIRING PUBLIC SERVANTS

I n our American republic, those who are the elected officials of the government are not rulers; they are public servants. In other words, they are the employees of the public, charged with assisting the public in the protection of their lives, liberties, and properties. To understand the concept of government, we can use a simple analogy.

Let's say that we have a town consisting of 100 people. Under the common law, each of these 100 people has the unalienable right to protect their own lives, liberties, and properties. This means that they individually and collectively have the right to use force, including deadly force, if necessary to protect their God-given, unalienable rights.

The town decides that they can better protect their rights by pooling their resources and hiring a security guard to patrol the town. Because they possess the right to protect themselves, they can delegate some of that responsibility to a security guard and hold their employee accountable for his or her performance at the job. They draw up a contract, delegating limited authority to their security guard to assist them in protecting themselves.

Now they have to find someone to fulfill the job. Several candidates apply and the citizens decide who to hire by voting. The candidate who receives the highest number of votes is selected for the position. However, in hiring this security guard, the citizens are not surrendering their unalienable right to protect their own lives, liberties, or properties. The security guard is their employee or public servant, hired under a contract which specifies his role is to protect them. Therefore, they, the public, are the source of the security guard's authority.

Granting Moral Consent

In American government, the essential idea is that town charters, state constitutions, and the federal constitution are the contracts under which our public servants are hired. These social contracts delegate limited powers to these public servants, which are always subject to the review of the "bosses," or "we the people." We hire these people as employees of "we the people" and they take office swearing to uphold their contract with "we the people." Their power is limited to protecting our unalienable rights because these are the only *just* powers we can delegate to them.

America is the only country in the world whose military and law enforcement does not swear allegiance to a government power. Instead, they swear allegiance to the Constitution, the contract under which they were hired. Again, the idea is that all those who work for the government have volunteered to be employees of "we the people" and thus to defend our unalienable rights.

When one looks at all of the evil actions undertaken by corrupt governments in the last century, and sees the tens of millions of people murdered and imprisoned for just disagreeing with their government, it is a sobering thought that these actions could not have taken place if a large percentage of the people had not given their moral consent by allowing the government to get away with these things. That's why we need to take a serious look at the issue of what we should and should not ask government to do.

Morality and the Delegation of Authority

Moral retribution, the harvest reaped by our actions under the law of the harvest, is not escaped by hiring another person to do your dirty work. If I pay someone to murder another human being, and they do so, both the hired gunman and I are guilty of murder. In fact, according to legal definition, we conspired to commit murder or, to put it another way, there was a "conspiracy to commit murder" and both of parties are equally guilty under the moral law.

Understanding this, let's return to our hypothetical community of 100 people who have hired a security guard to help protect them in their lives, liberties, and properties. There are two people in this community whom we will call Joe and Sarah. Sarah is financially well off, whereas Joe is not. Even though this is the case, as long as Sarah has derived her wealth from honest activities, she has an unalienable right to the wealth (property) she has acquired. If Joe breaks into Sarah's house and steals from her, he has committed a crime.

Because Joe has trespassed against Sarah's rights, Sarah can morally delegate the authority to the security guard to arrest Joe. He can then be tried and appropriate action can be taken to restore the peace and equity of the community. If the people of the community are just, then the appropriate action would be to compel Joe to make restitution to Sarah.

However, what would happen if the security guard took it upon himself to take Sarah's property and give it to Joe? In this case, the security guard would have committed the crime. Because he is a public servant, charged with protecting the life, liberty, and property of those who hired him, the security guard has violated the terms of his contract. He has become a criminal himself, since the people did not grant him this authority and Sarah has every right to seek to have him arrested and punished.

This is the nature of law in a republic. No one is "above the law," as everyone is subject to the same moral code. There are no rulers, only public servants; employees who assist the citizens in protecting their rights.

A Majority Vote Doesn't Make Something Moral

But this concept goes much further. What happens if a group of concerned citizens witness Joe's plight? Being concerned about his welfare, they create a referendum and ask the town to vote to authorize the security guard to take property from Sarah and give it to Joe. If enough people in the town are covetous or jealous of Sarah's wealth, they may actually win a majority vote and order their employee to take some of Sarah's money and give it to Joe.

Does this vote make the action moral? Does the number of people involved in an action have anything to do with its morality? I would argue that morality is not dependent on scale. If it's immoral for one person to do it, it's immoral for a million people to do it.

The number of people involved in a trespass against the life, liberty, or property of another has no effect on the moral nature of the act. If fifty-one people in our imaginary community get together and authorize the security guard they have hired to trespass against another person's property, then all fifty-one people have conspired to commit a crime. They are, in fact, co-conspirators. And, if the security guard obeys their orders and commits the crime, then the security guard is also equally guilty of this crime.

Of course, they will have the illusion that they are morally justified if they believe in "democracy," because the majority were in favor of the act. The problem is that the universal, inescapable "law of the harvest" still applies. It will swiftly and immediately require restitution on everyone who acted as part of the conspiracy, not just the security guard who "followed orders."

How can this be? Well, before this event, each member of the community was equal before the law. They lived with equity and, therefore, in peace. Now Sarah is angry because her unalienable right to property has been trespassed against. She also has friends and supporters and they are also angry. Those who voted for to "help" Joe will sense this anger and feel fear. They will realize that if Sarah and her followers can sway the majority opinion, they may be able to order the security guard to move against their liberty and property too.

Two parties have formed, each seeking to sway the majority to its point of view so they can gain control of the security guard. The peace has been broken. Liberty, founded in the moral principle of unalienable rights and the Golden Rule, has been violated. As soon as the rights of one member of the community were violated, the rights of all members of the community were put at risk.

Let me repeat that in a slightly different way. As soon as the government violates the unalienable rights of *any* citizen in a society, the equity has been broken and *every* member of that society's rights are at risk.

The Robin Hood Myth

The Robin Hood myth that permeates our culture is that taking from the rich (someone who has) and giving to the poor (someone who has not) is somehow moral. It is the idea that the ends justify the means. But the law of the harvest really tells us that the means creates the ends. An unjust means will not create a just end.

By the way, the story of Robin Hood is really about fighting against an unjust government, not against the rich. While the king is away, the corrupt leaders who have been left in charge are plundering the common people for the benefit of the social elite. Robin Hood is taking back (seeking restitution for) money unjustly taken from the poor by the government, not money honestly earned by wealthier citizens.

In a moral society, if a person has committed trespass against others, then we have a crime, which justifies seeking moral retribution as described in the previous chapter. But if someone has prospered through strictly voluntary transactions, which have benefited others in the process, it is immoral to covet their property and use force to take it away from them, even if we think it's for a "good cause."

The bottom line is that we cannot morally give consent to a government to perform functions we could not morally do ourselves. In fact, *we must not* if we want to reap a positive harvest of good in our own lives. If we ignore the moral law and give our moral consent for government to trespass against the rights of others, "we the people" are morally accountable and responsible for the crimes committed by the government. Therefore, "we the people" will reap the moral retribution required by the law of the harvest. This unpleasant crop is often referred to as "God's judgments."

We're seeing the results of our violating these principles in our country today. We have political parties, each striving to gain the will of the majority so they can force their ideas on the minority. This is not a free society; instead, it is a society where anger and fear are driving the people to seek to use government to force their ideas on others. The moral compass, set forth in the Declaration of Independence, is lacking in today's social fabric, which has corrupted the government, divided the people, and threatened to tear our country apart with civil unrest.

Our Moral Responsibility

How do we escape this moral problem? First, we need to realize that when we defend and support government actions that trespass against the unalienable rights of others, whether in this country or in other countries, we are entering a conspiracy to commit crime. This means that the "law of the harvest" will immediately take effect on our culture and society, causing us to live in anger and fear. In order to restore our own inner peace, we must first adopt moral principles that respect the unalienable rights of others.

Then, we need to withdraw our own consent by no longer lending support and approval to actions of government that trespass against the lives, liberties, or properties of others. We need to step up and start seeking a return to the principles of equity by promoting and defending the moral law. This includes demanding the government to follow "due process," which is described in the next chapter.

First, however, I want to stress again that the law of the harvest is universal and automatic. It will act on you whether you believe in it or not. It will also act on you whether you act on your own or you delegate someone else to act for you. This is where we all need to seriously repent as a nation, since almost everyone has bought into the idea of taking the wealth of others and allowing it to be redistributed. The arguments are generally over how it gets redistributed and not over the morality of the act of seizing it.

If we do not repent of this as a nation, the law of the harvest will continue to cause us to reap financial problems as a nation. Ultimately, if we continue to support this improper delegation of our moral authority, it will destroy both our economy and our country.

CHAPTER NINE

DUE PROCESS OF LAW

The public is supposed to maintain their primary authority in our republic through due process of law. This is stated in the Bill of Rights, which says that we cannot be deprived of life, liberty, or property, except by due process of law. Unfortunately, few people know what due process is, which is why due process has been all but destroyed in this country.

To explain due process, let's return to the idea that the people in government are employees or public servants. Due process is how the public is supposed to retain control over their servants.

If you had a security guard watching over your property, does he have the authority to become your boss? Of course not. But how do you prevent him from seizing authority over you he does not possess? That was reason for the Constitution of the United States and the Bill of Rights. It was supposed to help prevent the abuse of power by our public servants. It hasn't totally prevented it, but it has certainly acted to inhibit it.

Many Americans know the rights guaranteed by the first and second amendments to the Constitution. However, most of the amendments in the Bill of Rights deal with issues of due process of law. These amendments define how our government employees obtain the authority over one of their bosses.

It is in the following three stages of due process that the true power of "we the people" should be found. Unfortunately, this part of freedom was something we had already almost completely lost when I went to China in 1986 and is being lost more and more as the years go by. We need to both understand it and fight to restore it.

Due Process Step One: Arresting Someone

Since "we the people" are the sovereign authority and government officials are only the servants, our servants must obtain a warrant, based on probable cause, to search our property or detain (arrest) us in our normal activities. Since both the act of searching someone's property and the act of detaining them are trespasses against the liberty and property of another, there is supposed to be some sort of permission granted from *We the People* for this to occur.

Probable cause is needed to give warrant (or permission) for the government official to violate the rights of liberty or property according to the fourth amendment. Probable cause is received when one or more citizens issue a complaint under oath indicating that the person or persons in question have committed a crime. The accusation of trespass against the inalienable rights of another is the probable cause that warrants (or permits) the use of force. The accusers are supposed to go before a judge and make statements, under oath, that they have evidence that the accused person or persons have violated the rights of another by committing a crime.

As I pointed out in an earlier posting, the original definition of a crime was "a deliberate and willful trespass against the life, liberty or property of another, in which there is a demonstrable loss of life, liberty or property." So, one or more of the bosses (the people), must assure the judge that they can demonstrate there has been a loss of life, liberty, or property as a result of the actions of the accused.

In giving the right to the government to make an arrest or authorize a search under probable cause, the citizen has not surrendered her or his right to defend themselves. Ever hear of a *citizen's arrest?* As one of the sovereigns of government, if I observe a trespass in progress, I should have a legal right to step in and attempt to stop the trespass.

And, since the public servants are also citizens, they have the right to make an arrest if they witness a crime in process. In this case, the probable cause is their own accusation or testimony that they witnessed the crime, which they must also present to a judge to initiate the remainder of due process.

Of course, a false arrest is possible under a common law system. A false arrest would occur when the accusers lied about the facts in order to have a person arrested. Police can make false arrests when they accuse people of crimes they didn't commit or that actions, which aren't crimes, give them the authority to do so.

A person making false statements under oath is violating the ninth commandment, which declares we should not bear false witness against our neighbor. Such a person is also guilty of attempting to use the force of government to commit a crime. We've already established that a person who hires someone to do their dirty work is morally responsible for the consequences. Therefore, if a private citizen or a government employee like a police officer fabricates the probable cause, they are guilty of a crime. The crime is called perjury.

It is interesting to note that in Old Testament law, a person who was found to be guilty of perjury was subject to the same penalty that the accused would have received if convicted under the false charge. In other words, if a person provided false evidence and testimony to charge someone with murder, they would be held guilty for attempted murder. This is because they sought to use the power of the government to commit murder.

If this principle were applied in law today, police officers would be far less tempted to tamper with evidence or plant evidence in order to obtain a conviction. Knowing they could experience the same penalty they were trying to inflict on others if they were caught would help them reconsider their actions.

Due Process Step Two: The Grand Jury

Once the accused citizen has been arrested, they have the right to be brought to the court to face their accuser(s). They have the right to answer the charge that has been made against them and bring in witnesses to demonstrate their innocence. If the crime they are charged with is "infamous," or in other words, a felony punishable by death or more than a year in prison, they have the right to face their accuser(s) before a grand jury, as guaranteed in the fifth amendment.

The grand jury is a body of sovereign citizens, representatives of the sovereign *We the People*. These representatives hear the accusation (or charges) and the accused person's answer to the accusations. After hearing the evidence, the grand jury takes a vote to determine whether the government will be given permission to prosecute the person charged with the crime. This permission from *We the People* is called a *grand jury indictment*.

Under a grand jury indictment, the person is taken to trial in the name of the people. If I were being properly indicted here in Utah by a grand jury, the indictment would say, "The people of the state of Utah versus Steven Horne." An indictment reading, "The State of Utah versus Steven Horne" means it is the government that is accusing and trying me, and that they are acting without the authority of *We the People*.

This is a serious violation of due process, as defined in the Bill of Rights, which specifically states that *no one* can be made to answer for any infamous crime without a grand jury indictment (unless, of course, they waive this right). In other words, the state (i.e., government) is not supposed to be able to put me on trial for a serious crime without the permission of the people.

Under our common law traditions, the only issue that can be addressed directly by a judge (a government employee) is a misdemeanor. A misdemeanor is a less serious crime and may not even be a crime by the previous definition we cited. For example, it can be a violation of basic public decency; in other words, public misbehavior. Depending on the jurisdiction, examples of misdemeanors currently recognized in many areas are petty theft, prostitution, public intoxication, simple assault, disorderly conduct, trespass, vandalism, reckless driving, discharging a firearm within city limits, and public nudity.

Ideally, these standards should be determined on the community level, because a community (town or city) has the right to expect some basic decency in the behavior of its citizens. The traditional punishment for these kinds of offenses is fines, and only if a citizen repeatedly refuses to pay the fines or repeatedly violates the law could he or she be charged with a more serious offense.

But returning to the importance of the grand jury. A properly constituted grand jury is supposed to have the power to indict public officials too. This means that grand juries are supposed to be the watchdogs of government, having the ability to charge one of their employees with a crime and force them to stand trial for it.

This is important because everyone in a republic has to follow the same standards of law, including those serving in the government. Remember that in a republic there aren't supposed to be rulers or a ruling class. Only under a system of ruler's law are the rules different for the people and the leaders.

Due Process Step Three: Trial by Jury

The final part of due process is the trial by jury, as guaranteed by the sixth amendment. Again, a jury is a body of private citizens, representatives of *We the People*. It is the jury who is delegated the responsibility of determining whether a person should be deprived of life, liberty, or property, not the government.

This is critically important. The government (who are only the public servants) should never have the authority to deprive one of their sovereigns of their lives, liberties, or properties. Under a true common law system, only a group representing the sovereign authority has the right to make these decisions.

Unfortunately, we have largely surrendered this right and responsibility, along with many of our other "due process" rights under common law. We now allow numerous bureaucrats in the executive branch of government to charge you with a crime, determine if you are guilty, and levy fines and other punishments without this right of a jury trial. The government should not be allowed to have this power in a republic by the people, of the people, and for the people.

It takes the unanimous consent of all twelve members of a jury to convict a person. If only one person is convinced that the person is innocent of the crime of which they are accused, the jury is hung and the person is acquitted. The magic of this is that it's hard to get twelve people to agree on anything. So, if all twelve people believe the evidence points to a person's guilt, that's a good basis for depriving someone of life, liberty, or property.

To see how one person who is unconvinced of a person's guilt can sway a jury, watch the brilliant 1957 film, *Twelve Angry Men*. Eleven of the jurors are convinced the defendant is guilty, but one man stands out, questioning that judgment. In the end, he manages to persuade the entire jury that the defendant is innocent.

Jury Nullification: The Ultimate Power of the People

The importance of the jury goes far beyond the jury's ability to determine guilt or innocence. Juries have the right to decide both the facts and the law. The facts are the evidence suggested by the prosecution that the law was broken. The law means that the jury has the right to decide if the law is moral or not, and even if it is moral, is it moral to apply the law in this situation?

To make this clearer, *trying the law* means that the jury has the right to overturn the legislature and nullify the law. It's a principle called *jury nullification.* It is the power of the people to overturn the elected representatives in the legislature and nullify the laws they pass.

Just as it takes all twelve jurors to decide a person is guilty, it also takes all twelve jurors to decide if the law is immoral. If they all decide that the law is wrong and violates the unalienable rights of the defendant, they have the ability to render the law null and void. You probably knew that the Supreme Court has declared laws unconstitutional, but in actuality, the jury of twelve citizens has both the moral right and the moral responsibility to perform a similar task. I bet that's something you were never taught in public school.

More than any other part of due process, it is the principle of jury nullification that gives the people their moral power and authority to control the government. That's why no one teaches people that they have this right. It is the absolute affirmation that the power of government lies with *We the People.*

The Founding Fathers understood this well. In 1771, John Adams said "It is not only...[the juror's] right, but his duty... to find the verdict according to his own best understanding, judgment, and conscience, though in direct opposition to the direction of the court."[29] Thomas Jefferson told Thomas Paine in 1799, "I consider trial by jury as the only anchor yet devised by man, by which a government can be held to the principles of its constitution."[30] Then, in 1794, Chief Justice John Jay instructed the jury "You have nevertheless a right to take upon yourselves to judge of both, and to determine the law as well as the fact in controversy."[31] To learn more, check out the Fully Informed Jury Association (fija.org), who are trying to educate Americans about their rights as jurors.

---

[29] Diary entry February 12, 1771, reprinted in The Works of John Adams, 254-255 (C. Adams ed. 1850). (http://libertytree.ca/quotes/John.Adams.Quote.5846)

[30] http://americanjurypower.org/home/quotes2.php

[31] *Ibid.*

Due Process is in Serious Danger

If you've read this, it should be very clear our government no longer follows due process in much of what it does. Government officials write their own warrants. They search property and detain people without warrants. People are indicted in the name of the state, not the people. Juries are not informed of their rights of jury nullification. Grand juries are not investigating alleged wrongdoing on the part of government officials. In short, we have largely substituted a government based on ruler's law for one based on common law.

What's unfortunate is that when I have tried to explain these concepts to people, many have argued that such a system isn't workable. It appears that many people are perfectly comfortable surrendering their authority and allowing government officials to be rulers rather than public servants.

This is most unfortunate, because when *We the People* give our moral consent for government to decide who should be deprived of life, liberty, or property, we put ourselves in grave danger, as I have already described. Our nation as a whole reaps an undesirable crop when we surrender our sovereign status to those who are supposed to be our public servants.

Chapter Ten

Compassion, Mercy, and Forgiveness

S o far, I've discussed government and justice from the standpoint of trespass against unalienable rights. Now, I want shift gears away from restraining evil to the idea of doing good. The ideas of unalienable rights, the Golden Rule, and the Law of the Harvest also help us to understand what is good and moral.

Returning to the idea of restitution as the basis of justice, as described in chapter six, let me explain how a restitution-based justice system allows for compassion. When justice is restitution based, it not only makes the "punishment" fit the crime; it also creates the framework through which mercy can be shown and forgiveness granted.

To illustrate how this works, I will refer to the story to which I alluded earlier—the story of Jean Valjean in Victor Hugo's novel *Les Miserables*. The book is the basis for a Broadway musical and Hollywood movie of the same name. If you haven't seen the movie or play, or read the book, I highly recommend doing so.

For those of you unfamiliar with *Les Miserables*, here's the basic story. Jean Valjean was an out-of-work woodcutter. He lived with his sister and her child. They had no food and his sister's child was starving.

In desperation, Jean Valjean breaks a shop window and steals a loaf of bread. He is caught and sentenced to five years hard labor. Because he repeatedly tries to escape, he winds up serving for nearly twenty years.

Anyone with any sense of compassion could understand the forces which drove Jean Valjean to do what he did, and if we have compassion for the situation, it seems very harsh and unfair to force someone into hard labor for five years (let alone twenty) for a crime brought on by desperation for the plight of a child.

In fact, the punishment made things even worse. It not only destroyed Jean Valjean's life; it destroyed the life of his sister and her child. The injustice he experienced turned Jean Valjean into an angry and hardened criminal, and it did nothing to fix the broken window or replace the bread the shopkeeper lost.

If Jean Valjean had lived in a society with a restitution-based, common law legal system, his sentence would have been to pay the shopkeeper the value of two loaves of bread and two windows. Since Jean Valjean has no money, this might have been satisfied by him performing work for the shopkeeper until the debt was paid. Or, he might have been compelled to work elsewhere until the debt was paid. But whatever the arrangements, the demands of justice would be satisfied. The shopkeeper would have been compensated for his loss.

Jean Valjean could plead with the judge for mercy, but it is not the judge who has suffered a loss. If the judge, representing the power of government, doesn't require Jean Valjean to make restitution, then the judge is acting unjustly to the shopkeeper. He'd be telling the shopkeeper, "It was alright that Jean Valjean stole from you. I'm forcing you to give up your property for his sake."

So, where in this story is there any room for compassion? It takes a very cold and heartless person to not have empathy for the plight of Jean Valjean. He wasn't even stealing for himself; he was trying to save a child from starving.

Mercy cannot rob justice or justice ceases to exist. Understanding this is critical. Without robbing justice, there are two ways Jean Valjean can be shown mercy.

Forgiving Those Who Trespass Against Us

The victim has it within his or her power to show mercy and to forgive. In the story above, upon hearing the plight of Jean Valjean, the shopkeeper might have compassion on him and chose to show mercy by forgiving him his trespass.

By the law of justice (and the law of the harvest), the shopkeeper is morally entitled to compensation for the trespass against his unalienable right of property. However, he can choose to forgo that right, turning that which was lost into a gift. That's the true meaning of the word forgive. It's why the root of the word forgive is give.

The only one who can rightfully give someone anything is the one who owns the thing being given. The bread and the window, being the shopkeeper's property, can be voluntarily given to Jean Valjean so that no debt is owed. This is what forgiveness is really all about.

In forgiving someone, the victim is voluntarily giving what was lost to the perpetrator of the trespass. The victim is literally giving them the lost life, liberty, or property, dropping the need for restitution in order to restore equity to society. They restore equity by offering mercy.

This is vitally important and something I believe few people understand. Anyone who says, "I may forgive, but I will never forget," has not actually forgiven. Forgiveness doesn't just release the trespasser from the penalty of the law; it also releases all of the negative feelings in the victim.

How can you feel hurt and resentful over something you have given to another person in an act of love and kindness? To say that you still hold negative feelings toward a person you have forgiven means you haven't really forgiven them. You're still holding onto what was lost and still wanting some type of restitution.

An Example of Forgiveness

This understanding of forgiveness is demonstrated in a powerful way later in the story of *Les Miserables*. After being released from prison,

Jean Valjean has become a bitter and angry man. He is discriminated against because he is a former convict. He has a hard time finding work or shelter.

Taking compassion on him, the benevolent Bishop Myriel gives him shelter and food, setting out his fine silver for the benefit of his "honored guest." Jean Valjean repays him by getting up in the middle of the night and stealing the bishop's silverware.

Caught by the police, Jean Valjean claims that the bishop gave him the silver as a gift, but the police don't buy his story. They haul him back to the bishop, who, to Jean Valjean's surprise, says that not only was the silver a gift, but that in his haste, Jean Valjean had forgotten part of the gift. He had left behind the silver candlesticks that were part of the set.

After the police are dismissed, the bishop tells Jean Valjean that he has "bought his soul for God," and that he must use the silver to become an honest man. After Jean Valjean departs, his housekeeper questions him about the situation. His response is that he had too long withheld this silver from the poor.

Bishop Myriel had transformed an act of trespass into an act of love. His true forgiveness becomes the catalyst for Jean Valjean to make the change from his hardened criminal mindset to becoming a man who is generous and caring to others. This is an example of how mercy (which is an act of love) can be a transforming power in the lives of others.

The Saving Power of Mercy

The second way in which mercy can be offered without denying justice is for a third party to enter the picture. The third party, hearing Jean Valjean's plea for mercy because he has no money to pay, offers to intervene and satisfy the shopkeeper's demand for justice. This third party says to the shopkeeper, "I will pay Jean Valjean's debt and he will now owe me instead of you." In other words, he buys or purchases the social debt or obligation.

In doing this, the third party acts as a savior to Jean Valjean. He rescues him from a situation from which he is powerless to rescue himself, which is what a savior (saver or rescuer) does. This is also called an act of atonement. Atonement literally means at-one-ment. It is the power by which justice and mercy are both satisfied, resulting in a restoration of the equity or oneness of society.

The third party can now offer mercy to Jean Valjean. He can make Jean Valjean work for him until the debt is paid, either in part or full, or he can completely forgive Jean Valjean because the loss is now his to give away.

Government Cannot Be Merciful

If government is to be just, it cannot be merciful. In the story of Jean Valjean, the judge cannot forgive because the lost property was not his. If he allows Jean Valjean to go free because he feels sorry for him, he is robbing the shopkeeper of his just right of restitution.

When the judge (or the government) fails to compel restitution for trespass and acts to "forgive" the trespass, the responsibility (or what some people would call the "karma") now falls on the judge. Under the common law, the judge now bears the weight of the social debt. The demand for restitution, through the law of the harvest, falls on him. By allowing mercy to rob justice, he has failed to uphold equity in the society and the shopkeeper will no longer have respect for the law.

The Old Testament is filled with warnings about this. It warns judges, "You shall not pervert justice; you shall not show partiality, nor take a bribe, for a bribe blinds the eyes of the wise and twists the words of the righteous" (Deut. 16:19, NKJV). Without impartial justice, it would be impossible to "live and inherit the land that the Lord your God is giving you" (Deut. 16:20, NKJV). This is an important principle that Americans need to understand if we wish to keep our republic.

Compassion and Reconciliation

In *The Third Alternative* by Stephen R. Covey, there is a chapter, coauthored by Larry M. Boyle, devoted to overcoming the adversarial nature of our legal system and finding win/win alternatives to the traditional win/lose legal battles in which most people engage.[32] In this case, he is referring to civil law cases, rather than criminal law cases, but the principle is the same under a true common law system.

This chapter claims that Jewish law (the Old Testament system to which we are referring), "put a high value on compassion and reconciliation." This tradition comes from stories about Aaron, the brother of the lawgiver Moses, who "loved peace and pursued peace and made peace between people."[33]

According to the tradition, Aaron would seek out the parties in the dispute and listen carefully to their stories and their pain. He would do this with both sides in the dispute and then seek for ways that would create reconciliation between the parties. In keeping with that tradition, "The win-win solution is the ideal Jewish lawyers and judges aspire to."[34]

This is a far cry from our legal system where people battle each other in anger and frustration. Ultimately, even the winning party loses—loses time, energy, good feelings, and money spent on attorneys and legal fees. In contrast, if we had a restitution-based justice system, it could be operated more like a mediation between the parties, creating a settlement that didn't just result in "an eye for eye" restitution, but rather in forgiveness and reconciliation. It's certainly an idea to ponder.

Mercy and the Christian Message

For the reader who is a Christian, what I'm explaining in this chapter offers a powerful insight into the message and mission of Jesus. Jesus

---

[32] Stephen R. Covey, The Third Alternative (New York, NY: Free Press 2011) pp 247-275

[33] Covey, Third Alternative, p 259

[34] Covey, Third Alternative, p 260

didn't just die on the cross for our sins. He voluntarily suffered all of struggles, temptations, abuses, and torments, which mankind inflict on each other—hunger, thirst, fatigue, betrayal, abandonment, abuse, and even death.

If the shopkeeper in the story is unwilling to forgive, then Jesus shows that God does offer a third alternative, just as Dr. Covey's book suggests. God Himself is willing to act as the third party by offering Himself as the restitution for all our trespasses. Having the power to make up for all losses, even death, He is the judge who can also extend mercy.

But in doing this, there is condition. The Law of the Harvest must still be satisfied. Justice must still be served. Mercy is only offered upon condition that one becomes merciful. "Blessed are the merciful for they shall obtain mercy" (Matt. 5:7, KJV); "Forgive us our trespasses as we forgive those who trespass against us" (Matt. 6:12, KJV).

When we are released from our fate, as Jean Valjean was released by the mercy of Bishop Myriel, we must awaken to love and mercy for others. As we extend love and mercy toward others, the Law of the Harvest justly extends mercy and forgiveness to us. When one understands this, the message of Christianity takes on a new light.

This leads naturally into a discussion of how the force of love and compassion plays a vital role in a free society. The concept of unalienable rights doesn't just help us define freedom and what it means to commit a crime; it also defines what it means to do good.

All too often, political discord arises, not because of what is being done but because of what is NOT being done. In other words, people want the government to not just restrain the evil, but to also do good. That's why it's important to understand what it means to do good, as I discuss in the next chapter.

CHAPTER ELEVEN

DOING GOOD

The Golden Rule has a dual manifestation. The negative aspect is "Don't do something to others you wouldn't want them to do to you." I've pointed out how evil violates this rule. When we treat people in a way we wouldn't want to be treated, we violate their unalienable rights. As a result, justice and the law of the harvest require restitution. All this is the basis of what has been called the lesser law. It's the law of "Thou shalt not..." like the rules for treating others found in the Ten Commandments.

The positive aspect of the Golden Rule is a "Thou shalt..." admonition. It says, "Treat others the way you *wish* they treated you." If evil is violating the negative aspect of the Golden Rule, it is logical to assume that good can be defined as acting in accordance with this positive aspect of the Golden Rule.

In fact, if crime can be defined as "*deliberate* and *willful* **trespass** against the life, liberty or property of another," then doing good can be defined as its opposite, "a *voluntary* and *willing* **sacrifice** of one's life, liberty or property, which is done to uphold, protect and defend the life, liberty and property of another." Most people think they are good people because they don't violate the negative aspect of the Golden Rule, but not doing evil isn't the same as doing good.

Another way of saying this is that there are two laws, a lesser law and a higher law, which can be related to the Old Testament and the New Testament of the Bible. The Old Testament, while it contains positive affirmations of the Golden Rule, is more focused on the violation of the negative aspect of the Golden Rule. The Old Testament law, therefore, is primarily concerned with justice, which is the essence of the lesser law.

The New Testament, while it also has it's "Thou shalt not..." passages, is more focused on the positive aspect of the Golden Rule, which is related to the higher moral law of mercy (as discussed in the last chapter) and charity (discussed in this chapter). This is the law of love, which means that you don't just treat people the way they treat you, you treat them *better* than they treat you. It means doing good even for those who don't deserve it.

The Three Levels of Love

I was given an understanding about ten years ago which helped me understand this idea even better. It was a recognition that there are different levels of human morality, which are based on different levels of love. Unfortunately, the word love is used in English to refer to many different emotional states, which causes confusion about the nature of love. Recognizing that there are three fundamentally different kinds of love helps clarify what the nature of the higher law of mercy and charity versus the lesser law of justice.

To explain this concept, I will use the Greek words, eros, philia, and agape. As I'll explain, eros is the love of the self, which manifests as desire. Philia is the love of friends and family, which manifests as fairness, honesty, loyalty, and devotion. Agape is the selfless love of others, which manifests through forgiveness or mercy and charity or selfless service to others.

EROS: SELF-CENTERED LOVE

We all desire happiness, pleasure, comfort, and the gratification of our physical needs. To seek fulfillment for ourselves is an expression of self-love. There is nothing wrong with loving ourselves or with desiring good for ourselves, but self-love that doesn't respect the rights of others will lead people to trespass on the rights of others to get what they want.

To a person who is completely self-absorbed, love is only what benefits the self, gratifying the physical senses and the need for worldly pleasures. This type of love can be expressed by the Greek word eros, which is the root of our English world erotic. The erotic is associated with sexual desire, which is a strong human urge, but it's also a good term to describe the love for anything that benefits the self.

Desire sees nothing wrong with violating the unalienable rights of others to gain satisfaction. I can seduce someone to fulfill my need for sex, steal to satisfy my hunger or desire for material comforts, or deceive people to gain acceptance and recognition. In short, a person who knows only the erotic love of desire typically thinks that cheating, lying, stealing, or otherwise trespassing on the rights of others is fine as long as they can get away with it.

A person for whom eros is their only expression of love cannot do good in the world. They are an evil tree that brings forth bitter fruit for anyone who gets involved with them. Everything they do which appears to be "good" is done for completely self-serving reasons. If they do something "charitable," it is done to make themselves look good. When they do something "nice" for you, it is only a bribe, which they will use at a later date to try to manipulate you into doing something for them.

PHILIA: THE LOVE OF FRIENDS AND FAMILY

At some point, people have to "wake up" to the fact that they can't really get what they want if they don't give something in return. They have to start to respect the unalienable rights of others and recognize that a healthier way to get what they desire is to offer something valuable in return for what they want. Thus, they develop an enlightened self-interest and start to become honest and fair. We might also say that they begin to understand and follow the lesser law of justice.

For instance, they develop their abilities and skills at providing goods and services that benefit others. As they engage in honest labor, they are able to trade with others for the things they want. Instead of trying to fulfill their desire for sexual intimacy with many partners, they find someone they can love and respect and make a commitment to that person through marriage.

Thus, a just person is one who doesn't trespass against others but seeks to be fair and honorable in what they do. Their love recognizes the rights of other people, which is the essence of the philia level of love. They are devoted to their friends and families and offer support, kindness, and respect to those they care about.

When a person works to benefit others and receives pay for it, or when they show care for their friends and family and receive companionship from them, they are engaged in fair exchange. They are fulfilling the Law of the Harvest, sowing for the benefit of others and receiving just compensation for it.

However, a person who only knows this level of love may also have enemies, those with whom he does not share philia love. If the care they offer to friends and family is not returned, they will begin to experience resentment and may come to hate someone they formerly loved. So, their "giving" isn't really giving. It would be more accurate to call it investing. They invest their time, energy, and resources in others in the hope of getting something in return.

If you find yourself resenting someone you "love," it shows that the love you have for them is the philia kind of love. It's good on a certain level, but it's not the ultimate expression of either love or goodness. That level of love is agape love.

AGAPE: CHARITABLE LOVE

This brings us back to the definition I gave of the good "a voluntary and willing sacrifice of one's life, liberty or property to uphold, protect and defend the life, liberty and property of another." If I have an unalienable right to my own life, liberty, and property, then anytime I give up what is rightfully mine for the benefit of another, I am making a sacrifice. Sacrifice is the essence of agape love, but not the self-martyring idea of sacrifice.

Self-martyrdom is a pretended agape love that is really a disguised desire for philia love. In the Sermon on the Mount, Jesus stressed that if we do our "good works" to be seen of others (and hopefully appreciated by them), we already have our reward. That is to say, our just compensation for publicly giving to a charity or performing public service is the publicity we receive for it.

Agape love causes us to give our lives, liberties, or properties to aid others *without expecting anything in return*. In fact, it's a love that is so selfless that one isn't really aware that one is "doing good." The left hand (the receiving hand) isn't even aware of what the right hand (the giving hand) is doing. Or, as Jesus expressed in His parable of the sheep and the goats, when the righteous are told about the good they have done, they ask, "When did we do these things?" (Mat. 25:37 KJV)

Agape was originally translated in the Bible into the English word charity. Although many modern translations use the word love instead, I think this doesn't convey a correct understanding of agape, as for most people love is either eros or philia or a mixture of both. In trying to teach people to express this love, Jesus told people to "love their enemies" and pray for those who treat them poorly. Why? So they can emulate the love of the heavenly Father (the Creator) who gives rain and sunshine to everyone equally. (Mat. 5:43-44 KJV)

Agape love gives because there is a need and does not ask the question, "What's in it for me?" To paraphrase what Jesus taught, if we love those who love us, what's so special about that? Everybody loves those who love them. (Mat. 5:46 KJV) Even those who only know the eros level of love desire the companionship of those who benefit them.

Love is a Gift, Not an Obligation

True charity is the act of giving of the self. People may give their property to help those who are less fortunate. They may also give of their liberty by donating their time and energy to assist others in need. They may even give their lives in the defense of the life, liberty, or property of others, which is the highest expression of love one can make. As Jesus taught, there is no love greater than the willingness to lay down one's life for others. (John 15:13 KJV)

Society recognizes willing sacrifice of property, liberty, and life as heroic, but there is no way to force someone to perform an act of charity (agape love). A sacrifice of life, liberty, or property that was coerced, as opposed to voluntary, means that the act was done out of eros or philia, not agape love. If I'm taxed to take care of the poor, I pay my taxes out of a desire to avoid punishment by the government, which is an interest in self-preservation. If I give money because of social pressure, so I'll look good in the eyes of my friends and family, the motive was philia, not agape love.

Likewise, if I make the sacrifice reluctantly, resenting what I "have" to give, or wondering, "what's in this for me?" then my unwillingness also means I have not performed a genuinely charitable act. The act was not done solely for the benefit of others; it is tainted with self-interest.

To put it more bluntly, Christmas presents or Valentine gifts to one's spouse are generally not true gifts. One gives in these circumstances because it's expected. It's a social obligation and, therefore, an expression of philia, the love expressed by duty and devotion. A true gift has no "strings" attached, and the receiver doesn't feel entitled to it, or at the very least isn't expecting it.

In fact, there is no *just* reason why anyone should be forced to put his/her own life, liberty, or property in danger to rescue another person. Trying to force people to do so is actually a trespass against them. This is the same principle expressed in the previous chapter, which is that mercy cannot rob justice. Charity can't rob justice either, which is why government (which is based on the use of force) can't be charitable.

There is no Such Thing as Government Charity

There's a saying I remember hearing as a child: "You can't legislate morality." What this really means is that government can't be used to do good in the world. To put it bluntly, you can't use force to make people to be good, not on the agape level at least.

People who see a problem in society and want the government to fix it are saying that other people should be *forced* to sacrifice their lives, liberties, and properties to solve this problem. This is not the same as seeing a problem in society and deciding to voluntarily do something to try to help fix it out the goodness of my own heart using my own life, liberty, or property.

I emphasize this because a society can theoretically be just, but not good. Justice is a necessary foundation to enable the good, but unless people are morally good, a free and just society is not likely to endure.

Under the law of justice, we can justly dismiss other people's problems, especially those created by their own choices, as "none of my business." But the positive expression of the Golden Rule asks us to put ourselves in their positions. If we are in a bad situation and need assistance, how would we want others to treat us? Would we want justice, or would we hope for mercy? I think most of us would hope someone would be merciful to us.

As I see it, people on the left of the political spectrum often see the poor and those that are in need and believe that the government should help them. They don't trust that people are good enough to help them without being coerced to do so.

People on the right sometimes appear callused and insensitive when they claim that this is not a proper role of government. And some people on this side of the political spectrum are overly caught up in the lesser law of justice and may be failing to see the need for the higher law of mercy.

I believe that reconciling justice and mercy within a society and becoming absolutely clear about the different kinds of love and the proper role of force in a society is needed in order to bridge this gap. So, my goal in the next chapters is to explain the role of government in creating economic opportunity for everyone and why free enterprise is essential to prosperity. I'll also explain why I think that the modern capitalistic money system is immoral and what we need to do to correct it.

Chapter Twelve

Free Trade and Just Weights and Measures

A huge part of the loss of freedom in America has been in the destruction of our unalienable rights to property. This has happened largely because most Americans do not understand economics. I believe this lack of understanding is deliberate, as a lack of understanding in this area allows people to be more easily manipulated and controlled. The systematic violation of the right of property has caused numerous problems in our society, but unfortunately, people have been taught to blame these problems on the free market and believe that the solution is more government control over our right of property.

Before I can begin to explain how our unalienable right of property has been systemically destroyed, I need to provide a mini lesson in economics. People won't be able to see how they are being cheated out of their property rights if they don't understand the moral foundations of what we call the free market. Later, I'll explain how our modern capitalistic system is not a true free market, but first let's understand the nature of free trade and then explain why it depends on a system of just weights and measures.

Human Specialization

Human society benefits from specialization. It's difficult for small groups of people to provide everything they need to sustain life and health, and next to impossible for a single person to do so. A team can accomplish more than a single individual, because each member of the team can use his/her strengths and abilities to compensate for the weaknesses and lack of ability in other members of the team. The incredible level of wealth and prosperity we enjoy, compared to people of the past, is entirely due to this specialization and the ability to exchange the goods and services we create with others.

My technical writing teacher in college put it to us this way. He asked, "Do you want to know the degree to which you are a master of technology or a slave to it?" In response to our guesses, he said, "How much of it can you recreate if you were stranded alone and naked on a desert island?" As someone who likes to watch survival shows, and has dabbled in outdoor survival and primitive skills, I know that the average person would struggle just to be able to survive and perhaps would not survive at all.

Do you have all the skills to make your own tools, build your own shelter, make clothing to protect you from the elements, hunt or gather food, start a fire without matches or fire starters, purify water and take care of yourself if you get injured or sick? Probably not. But, if you have a team of people, each of whom have skills in one or more of these areas, your chances of not only surviving but also thriving would increase dramatically.

The Body of Humanity

I point this out to illustrate why the level of specialization we have achieved in modern society is essential to lifting the health, prosperity, and happiness of mankind in general. We are very dependent on each other. So dependent in fact that humanity as a whole could be thought of as a greater living organism, an analogy used in the Bible to illustrate how believers should treat each other. (See 1Cor. 12:14-19.)

As someone who has studied natural health care for decades, I wish to borrow from this analogy to discuss human economics. Every cell in the body is an individual life form that can live, reproduce itself, and die. Yet, it is also part of the greater whole. Each cell needs food, oxygen, a regulated temperature, water, and the removal of waste materials to survive, but it is dependent on the rest of the body to get these things.

The cells of the body have become differentiated, forming tissues, organs, and systems, each of which is contributing something to the good of the body as a whole. The lungs supply oxygen and remove carbon dioxide waste. The digestive system supplies nutrients. The blood and lymph circulate nutrients and remove wastes. The colon and kidneys also remove wastes.

All of this specialization allows us to do things a single cell could never do, just as specialization and trade among human beings allows humanity to achieve more than any single individual ever could. The fact is that we need each other just to have some of the simplest things we take for granted every day. The book and video, *I Pencil*, explain this concept very well. I encourage you to read the book; it's free online.[35] You can also search for the video *I, Pencil* on YouTube.

Barter and Economics

When I voluntarily create something of value for others and voluntarily trade it to receive something of value for myself, I am engaging in barter. People have bartered with each other throughout recorded history. Barter is the fundamental essence of economics and when barter is honest or fair and voluntary, it raises everyone's standard of living.

Let's say that I'm very good at raising sheep and you're very good at growing wheat. You need wheat and I need sheep, so we make a trade and we both benefit. However, there are limitations to this kind of direct exchange. I might want your wheat, but you may not want my sheep. This problem is solved by creating a medium of exchange, which is also called money.

---

[35] https://fee.org/resources/i-pencil/

At its most fundamental nature, money is a commodity that has fairly universal value, which can be used as a go-between or medium to make barter easier. I can trade the sheep I produce for money and then trade the money for the wheat I need.

Theoretically, anything could be used as a medium of exchange (diamonds, other precious gemstones, seashells, beads, slips of paper with writing on them, or even numbers in a computer). However, in Western societies, precious metals, particularly gold or silver, became the preferred medium of exchange. While gold and silver aren't directly necessary for human life (you can't eat them, wear them, or use them for shelter), they are relatively rare, don't spoil or deteriorate, and are relatively light and easy to transport from one place to another.

To make it easier to trade with gold and silver, people started to make coins out of them and these coins were traditionally considered money. Coins were a way of quickly identifying the amount of gold or silver being traded, as the coins were stamped with some type of official image and the value (amount) of gold or silver they contained. This brings us to the importance of having a system of standard weights and measures.

Standard Weights and Measures

All barter, with or without a monetary system, requires the use of a system of weights and measures. This is required because we need to know how much of something we're getting in a trade and the other person knows how much we're giving in exchange.

If I'm paying $3.00 for a gallon of milk, I want to know that I'm getting the same amount of milk each time I buy it. A person who puts less than one gallon in the jug or dilutes the milk with water is cheating me. They are committing an act of theft by deceit. When we make trades, we want to know that we're getting what we bargained for, not something different than was agreed.

In ancient times people, weighed things using a balance scale. You had weights that you could put on one side of the scale. You then put the commodity being traded on the other side. When the scale balanced, you knew you had a certain weight of that commodity because the scale balanced.

Just weights and measurements are an established requirement of the common law. For example, Lev. 19:35-36 (NKJV) says, "You shall do no injustice in judgment, in measurement of length, weight, or volume. You shall have honest scales, honest weights." Prov. 20:10 (NKJV) stresses the same idea: "Diverse weights and diverse measures, they are both alike, an abomination to the Lord."

Finally, the prophet Amos spoke of the corrupt merchants who in selling their wheat sought to make the ephah (something like our modern bushel) small and the shekel (coin) great and to cheat with dishonest scales (Amos 8:5 NKJV). In other words, he was condemning the seller who through dishonest weights and measures gave the buyer less grain than he paid for. In short, under the common law, we all know that it's wrong to cheat in a trade because we ourselves don't like to be cheated.

Honest, free exchange is not a violation of the common law and, therefore, can never be a crime. It becomes a crime, however, when people try to get unjust gains, when they don't deliver what was agreed upon by using inferior materials, deceptive practices, and unjust weights and measures. This isn't true just for the goods and services being traded; it's also true in regard to the medium of exchange being used to make trade easier, which brings us back to the use of gold and silver as money.

Constitutional Standards and Money

As previously explained, coins were made to contain a specific amount of gold or silver with the value (weight) stamped on the coin. The rough edges to coins were to prevent people from scraping small amounts of gold or silver off the coin to make it smaller. Honest coining of money is part of having a just system of weights and measures. If I'm using gold or silver coins as a medium of exchange, I need to know how much gold or silver I actually have.

The Constitution of the United States gave Congress the power to establish both a monetary system and a system of standard weights and measures in Article 8. It said Congress had the power "To coin Money, regulate the Value thereof, and of foreign Coin, and fix the Standard of Weights and Measures."[36] The fact that both of these powers are delegated in the same clause shows they are related to each other.

Americans were already using the traditional English system of weights and measures (ounces, pounds, pints, gallons, feet, miles, etc.) and this was allowed to stand without Congress making any changes. However, the Treasury Department established standards for these weights and measures beginning in the late 1830s when they sent a complete set of weights and measures to each state.

As for the monetary system, the value set by Congress was the dollar, a unit of measurement that refers to a silver coin containing 371.25 grains of fine silver, which is slightly less than one ounce. The term dollar in reference to gold and silver is the same as the use of the term caret in gemstones. A carat is approximately two hundred milligrams (0.2 grams) or one fifth of a gram. Thus, both terms, dollar and caret, are measurements of weight.

Congress regulated the value of gold to silver by establishing silver coins as having a 15 to 1 ratio to gold coins. That is, one grain of gold was equivalent to 15 grains of silver. Thus, the original constitutional money, established by Congress, consisted of three gold coins (the Eagle or $10 gold piece, the half eagle and the quarter eagle) and five silver coins (the dollar, half dollar, quarter dollar, dime and nickel). There were also two copper coins, the cent and the half cent.

---

[36] Constitution of the United States, Article 8, Clause 5

Manipulating Money

I've just described why a uniform standard of weights and measures, including honest measurement of the value of the money, is a foundational necessity for an honest economic system. Unfortunately, governments have a long history of tampering with a society's money system. Unjust governments debase the value of the money to steal the wealth (property) of their citizens. Here's how this has been done in the past.

Governments of other countries, both past and present, established a standard measure for gold and silver coins, just like America. For example, ancient Roman coins included the talent and the denarius. More modern examples are the pound (English), franc (French), and the Yuan (China). Although the value (weight) of these coins were different, trading with them should be rather straightforward. All one would have to do is to know the value for the coin in question and convert that into the money system with which one is familiar. It's no more difficult than converting a measurement given in imperial measures to one given in metrics.

But governments made this process more complex by establishing the concept of a legal tender. That is, only coins made within the country (and bearing the image of the current ruler) were legal. Thus, coins had to be exchanged in order to be used in international trade, and this was always done by the moneychangers (or bankers) who charged a fee for the service.

By having a legal tender, when a new king (or government) came to power, they could recall all the old coins and require they be melted down and coined again with the image of the new king on the coin. However, when the new coins were made, they were often made slightly smaller or were diluted with other metals so that they contained less gold or silver than before. Nevertheless, the stamp on the coin gave it the same value. This enabled the new government to inflate the supply of money by minting more coins (claiming they had the same value) out of the same amount of precious metal.

If you think about this using any other standard weight or measure, you can readily see how dishonest this is. Let's just suppose that I had the power to recall all gallons of milk, then either dilute them with water or reduce the amount of milk in each gallon. I could now put them all into the marketplace claiming that all of these new "gallons" were equivalent to the old gallon and keep the surplus milk for myself to sell. When put in these terms, one can see how deceptive such a practice would be. After all, it would be very unfair to make people pay the same price for the old gallon as the new one, wouldn't it?

Debasing Money Creates Inflation

Whoever has the power to debase the money system has the power to increase their wealth at the expense of everyone else. At first, the debased money has the same buying power as the old money, but this doesn't last forever. The value of the money diminishes, causing prices to go up. Inflation isn't caused by increases in the value of the goods and services we purchase. It's caused by a decrease in the value of the money used to purchase them.

To understand this better, imagine you have a balance scale, like the one pictured on the next page. On one side you have all of the goods and services available for purchase. This is the value people seek. On the other side you have all the money that can be used as a medium of exchange to trade for these goods and services. This scale always seeks balance, so if you add more money to the scale but the quantity of goods and services available to purchase remains the same, then people will bid up the price of the goods and services to keep the scale balanced.

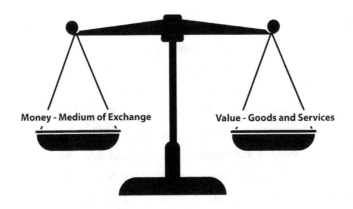

Let me illustrate with a practical example. Let's say I'm selling a home and I'm asking $400,000 for it. If money to buy homes is in short supply, people may come and make an offer to buy it for less than the price I'm asking. Maybe they'll offer me $380,000. If I can't find a buyer for the original amount, and I really need to sell the house, I may agree to the lower price. Thus, the price goes down because the medium of exchange is in short supply. That's called deflation.

On the other hand, if there is a lot of money available to buy homes, I might have two buyers who both want my home. One offers me my asking price, but the other has more money and offers me a higher price. They offer $420,000. I accept the higher offer, which means the price of the home just went up. That's called inflation.

In reality, the value of my home (from a strictly utilitarian point of view) isn't going up or down. The price depends on the availability of money to exchange for it. More money, higher prices. Less money, lower prices.

If you don't already understand this concept, it's very important that you grasp it, so stick with me. People are so blinded by the idea of having money that they fail to grasp the most fundamental truth of economics, which is, people don't really want money; they want goods and services. They only value money because it can be used to barter for what they want. If the medium of exchange is debased to the point that it loses value and people no longer want to accept it in trade for their goods and services, it becomes worthless. Like any commodity, money only has value as long as people accept it as a means of exchange.

One of the reasons the Roman Empire fell apart was because of the debasing of its currency. Many countries have also collapsed, following the monetary system failing. I point all this out only because our government and banking systems have been debasing our currency for decades, something that is causing more and more economic hardships for the American people. And, if we don't recognize this and return to an honest money system, our civilization will also collapse. I'll explain more about how this is happening in the next chapter.

CHAPTER THIRTEEN

THE FRAUD OF TRADING DEBT AS MONEY

In chapter six, I explained how our American system fails to follow the common law in its understanding of justice. I explained that justice is based on compelling the person committing a trespass to make compensation to the victim. In this chapter, and the ones that follow, I want to show some other ways in which America failed to implement the common moral law. I also want to explain how this failure is being used to deceive us and destroy our freedom and rights of property.

Some of our Founding Fathers recognized what I am about to explain. For instance, John Adams, in a letter written to Thomas Jefferson in 1787, said, "All the perplexities, confusion, and distress in America arise, not from defects of the Constitution, not from want of honor or virtue, so much as from downright ignorance of the nature of coin, credit and circulation."[37]

In the last chapter, I discussed how a uniform standard of weights and measures is essential to free trade. I also talked about how governments of the past debased the value of gold and silver coins, which lead to inflation and, in many cases, the monetary collapse and downfall of civilizations.

---

[37] John Adams, Letter to Thomas Jefferson, August 25, 1787, http://www.quotation-spage.com/quote/41388.html

There's a limit to how much you can debase a currency based on gold and silver, but there is virtually no limit to how much you can debase a medium of exchange that is nothing more than paper or numbers in a computer. Daniel Webster recognized this when he said, "Of all the contrivances devised for cheating the laboring classes of mankind, none has been more effective than that which deludes him with paper money."[38]

We often hear people praise capitalism and equate it with a free market or free enterprise system. However, I don't agree that our current capitalistic society is a genuine system of free enterprise. It can't be because, as I am about to point out, we do not have an honest money system and without an honest money system, there is no such thing as completely free trade.

Those who criticize the capitalistic economic system do so claiming it makes the rich, richer and the poor, poorer. They are absolutely correct, but err in thinking this is caused by free markets, and that government control of free market is the solution. I've been in many foreign countries and what I see is that the opposite is taking place. In countries where government controls the economy, the division between rich and poor is even greater than it currently is in America. So we first have to understand what the problem really is, which is what I want to do in this chapter.

Bank Notes and Paper Money

Let's begin by examining the origins of paper money. People have always had to guard their property against those who would steal it from them. Gold and silver coins are heavy and hard to carry around in any large quantity. They also need to be stored. To solve this problem, people created vaults where people could place their gold and silver (and other

---

[38] Mr. Webster's Speeches in the Senate Upon the Question of Renewing the Charter of the Bank of the United States (ed. 1832), https://libquotes.com/daniel-webster/quote/lbi1w7y

valuables) for safekeeping. It makes perfect sense that people would be willing to pay someone who could help guard their valuables.

A person depositing his/her gold or silver into the vault will need a receipt. The vault, which I'll refer to hereafter as the bank, issues the receipt in the form of a note. A note is also known as a *promissory note* because it is a promise to pay something to someone. Legally, a promissory note has four parts. It says *who*, will pay *what, to whom,* and *when.* So, when a person would deposit his/her gold and silver at the bank, the bank would give the person a promissory note as a receipt. The bank note would say something to the effect that the bank (who) will pay to the bearer (to whom) 1, 5, 10, 30 or 100 dollars in silver or gold (what) on demand (when). The note is evidence that the bank owes the bearer a debt.

When a person wanted to redeem the note and collect the gold or silver, they took the note to the bank, which was then obligated to give them the gold or silver. People found it much easier to trade these notes as payment for goods and services than gold or silver coins. Thus, the notes themselves were circulated *as if* they were money. People accepted the paper notes as money because they assumed they could take them to the bank and redeem them for the actual gold and silver coins.

Savings Accounts and Loans

None of this would be problematic if it weren't for the next step taken by the bank. The bank didn't just store the gold or silver; it used the gold and silver as a backing for debts in the form of loans. This use of the deposited money for loans is part of our current capitalistic economic system. I'll explain capital and the problems with charging interest on monetary loans (something traditionally called usury in the Bible) in the next chapter, but for now let's just concentrate on the nature of the loans.

Instead of having people pay the bank to store their gold and silver, the bank offered people interest on their money in exchange for the bank being able to loan it to other people. This seems like a good idea were it not for the idea that people didn't fully understand that they were putting their money at risk.

They were still trading the notes that told them their gold and silver money was still in the bank, but it wasn't. Most of it had been used to back loans to other people. So, the people who had received the loan had the money, while the people holding the bank notes for their deposits thought they still had the money.

For ease of discussion, let's say that someone deposits $1,000 in gold coins in the bank. The person receives $1,000 worth of bank notes promising to return the gold, which they start circulating as money. Now, let's say the bank issues a loan for 90 percent of that amount. So, they issue a loan for $900. The person deposits the $900 in gold coins into the bank and receives $900 in bank notes. So, although the bank only has $1,000 in actual gold, there are now outstanding notes for $1,900 worth of gold being traded in the community.

Of course, the loan is probably secured, meaning that some form of property was pledged as collateral, such as a home, car, or business. So, if the borrower defaults on payments, the bank can seize the property and sell it to recover their money. However, the fact remains that only a fraction of the actual gold originally deposited in the bank is available to cover the notes. So, as long as neither the original depositor or the person who received the loan don't actually try to redeem the notes, everything is fine. The borrower eventually pays back the loan, with interest, and the bank shares that interest with the depositor.

Nevertheless, the "money supply" has been artificially inflated by this process. One thousand actual dollars of gold have now become one thousand, nine hundred paper dollars. Thus, the banking process actually debases the money supply and creates inflation, particularly in the assets used to secure loans.

Leveraging Assets

The problem is much worse than what is described above. Why? Because the borrower deposits the loan he received back into the bank. Since the loan is often secured by some type of asset (such as a home or a business), these notes are now assets, which the bank can leverage as the basis for more loans.

The assets used to secure the loans are called capital. Banks leverage their capital by issuing loans against it. A financially healthy bank is typically leveraged around ten or twelve to one. If we were still using a gold standard, what this actually means is that for every dollar of gold the bank actually held, there would be bank notes outstanding (in the form of secured and unsecured loans) to the tune of ten to twelve dollars.

Thus, through trading notes (debt) as if it were money, the banking system could literally turn $1,000 of actual physical money (gold or silver) into $10,000 to $12,000 of bank notes. As long as they held enough capital reserves to redeem the notes that were actually turned in, the system continues to function and nobody would notice the debasement of the currency because they don't recognize the source of the inflating prices of homes, cars, and other assets the bank is leveraging to create loans.

However, if people began to lose faith in the value of the notes, there would be a "run on the bank." The bank couldn't redeem the notes unless it seizes the leveraged assets, so it has to close its doors and perhaps declare bankruptcy. Thus, the people would lose all inflated value of the paper notes. This causes a drop in prices and a shortage of money, something known as a financial depression.

The Debasing of the American Money System

Claiming to "solve" the problem of banks going insolvent, the Federal Reserve was incorporated as a privately held bank under the authorization of the United States government. The Federal Reserve was given control over all the banks in the United States and paper notes became even more widely used as if they were money. However, the notes were still, theoretically at least, backed by gold and silver. For example, I still have an old silver certificate, which says "the United States Treasury (who) will pay to the bearer (to whom) one dollar silver (what) on demand (when)."

Then, in 1933, the government acted to safeguard the banking system (which was over leveraged and in danger of collapsing due to people wanting to redeem their notes for gold). They passed a law that gave the secretary of the Treasury the power to require all individuals and corporations to hand over all their gold coin, gold bullion, or gold certificates (gold bank notes) as it was necessary to protect the currency system in the United States.[3940]

Americans continued to have silver coins until 1965, when President Lyndon Johnson signed a bill removing silver coins from circulation. They were replaced with coins made from copper and nickel.[41] The problem arose because the value of the paper dollar had declined so much that one dollar of silver was worth more than the paper dollar, so people were keeping the coins instead of circulating them.

In 1971, Richard Nixon completely removed the gold backing of any United States paper money.[42] This was another milestone in the debasement of the American monetary system. Since the creation of the Federal Reserve, the American "dollar" has lost 96 percent of its

---

[39] Thomas E. Woods, Jr., "The Great Gold Robbery of 1933," https://mises.org/library/great-gold-robbery-1933

[40] Daniel Carr, "FDR's 1933 Gold Confiscation was a Bailout of the Federal Reserve Bank," http://www.moonlightmint.com/bailout.htm

[41] Jill Westeryn, "One Hundred Years of Silver Dollar Coinage (1878-1978)," April 15, 2021, https://www.usmint.gov/news/inside-the-mint/one-hundred-years-of-silver-dollar-coinage-1878-1978

[42] "Nixon Ends Convertability of U.S. Dollars to Gold and Announces Wage/Price Controls," August 1971, https://www.federalreservehistory.org/essays/gold-convertibility-ends

value. Documentation of this information can easily be found on the internet.[43][44] My focus here is to point out that this really means that 96 percent of the wealth of ordinary Americans has been stolen by this corrupt and immoral monetary system.

Federal Reserve Notes are Instruments of Debt

If one examines a Federal Reserve note, one will quickly be able to see that all the traditional characteristics of a promissory note have been removed. Instead of saying who will pay what to whom and when, it simply says, "This note is legal tender for all debts public and private." The understanding of the dollar as a unit of measurement is gone.

To see how ridiculous this is, let's suppose that I give you a "note" that says, Steven Horne agrees to pay the holder of this note, on demand, one gallon. The question would rapidly arise, a gallon of what? Water, gasoline, oil, milk? The term gallon is meaningless if we don't know what substance I'm offering you a gallon of.

The same is true for the term dollar. The illusion of money, which has been fostered on just about the entire populous is that a piece of printed paper has some kind of inherent value. Since a dollar is a measurement, we need to know what we have a dollar of—gold, silver, copper, nickel, tin? It makes a difference.

However, in reality, we have a dollar of nothing. In fact, when one dissects what the modern dollar is, we're actually trading in debt. We're actually giving someone a debt, owed to the Federal Reserve, in exchange for goods and services.

In unpacking this, I first need to explain what a *tender* is. Referring back to the example of barter I made earlier, let's suppose I offered you five bushels of wheat in exchange for one sheep. The bushels of

---

[43] "Visusalizing the Purchasing Power of the Dollar Over the Last Century," https://howmuch.net/articles/rise-and-fall-dollar

[44] David Lee, How Much Value has the U.S. dollar lost since 1913? The answer might surprise you," April 16, 2020, https://dreadopedia.com/2020/04/16/how-much-value-has-the-u-s-dollar-lost-since-1913-the-answer-might-surprise-you/

wheat are the *tender* I'm making for the exchange. In other countries, you often haggle with merchants over the price. They ask for an overly inflated price and you make a lower tender. They counter with a lower price and you negotiate until you tender a price they accept.

In other words, a tender is an offer of payment. If we translate what the Federal Reserve note is saying, it literally means, "This promise to pay (note) is a legal offer of payment." It isn't a payment; it's an offer of payment and the payment is a note, which is a promise to pay. Confusing? It's intended to be because it's a deception and it gets worse because Federal Reserve notes are not put into circulation; they are loaned into circulation.

Debt Slavery

What this means is that every dollar you have is not a note; it is actually a bill. When you get a bill in the mail, are you getting a promise to receive something or a notice that you need to pay something? We all know that a bill is a paper that says you owe something, right? So, that's why they are called dollar *bills*.

You have to realize that the Federal Reserve notes you hold aren't your property. They belong to the Federal Reserve. They were loaned into circulation, which means they are owed back to the Federal Reserve. What's worse, they were loaned with interest.

This means that all the money in circulation is owed to the Federal Reserve with interest. The problem is that if everyone returned all the paper money to the Federal Reserve, they would still owe the interest to the Federal Reserve. But how could the debt ever be repaid, then? It can't, because the total amount of debt owed to the Federal Reserve exceeds the total amount of Federal Reserve notes in circulation. As I was writing this, a quick internet search revealed that there are about 21 billion in Federal Reserve notes in circulation[45] with over 28 tril-

---

[45] https://www.federalreserve.gov/paymentsystems/coin_currcircvolume.htm

lion dollars in public debt[46] and over 14 trillion in household private debt.[47] These figures do not include business debt and will have likely increased substantially by the time you read this book.

What this means is that there simply isn't enough paper money in the entire country to even begin to pay all the debt. Thus, the only way to keep the economy afloat is to continue to inflate the money supply and loan more money into existence, creating more debt and higher prices. This has been called debt slavery.

One you understand this, you will readily see why the rich get richer and the poor get poorer. You can also readily see why the entire system is an immoral scam.

The Capitalistic Banking System is Immoral

Just think about it. If you had $100 in gold coins and were able to issue promissory notes as loans for $1,000 worth of loans based on your $100 worth of gold coins, you'd really have a racket going, wouldn't you? Let's also imagine that at some point your racket starts to be exposed because you can't redeem all the notes. So, with the force of government backing you, you're able to say nobody has a right to your gold; they just need to accept your notes as money. Now, you can create money out of thin air and put it into circulation as much as you'd like (maybe with a little government oversight, but that's not a big problem since the government borrows from you too).

When put in this light, we can readily see that the entire system is immoral and unfair. It completely violates the principle of honest weights and measures and a free market where people can honestly exchange goods and services. Just on that basis alone, the entire system could be taken down and replaced with an honest one anytime the people woke up and realized what was being done to them. I believe the

---

[46] https://www.thebalance.com/the-u-s-debt-and-how-it-got-so-big-3305778

[47] https://www.debt.org/faqs/americans-in-debt/demographics/

real solutions lie in a return to Old Testament principles of common law, which I discuss in the next chapter.

Chapter Fourteen

Solutions to the
Weaknesses of Capitalism

I've pondered the economic aspect of freedom for many years, and I've come to the conclusion that the current capitalistic system has two fundamental flaws which allow wealth (and the power that goes with it) to gradually accumulate in the hands of a few. But before I explain these two principles, I need to give another mini lesson in economics.

As customers give a business their money in exchange for the goods and services, the business acquires money. The money not used for operating expenses or paid to the owners is capital, which can be invested into creating further means of production. It takes capital to buy equipment and other resources needed to get a business started and to expand its operations.

If a person doesn't have enough capital to start or expand a business themselves, they can raise capital by getting other people to invest in the business. When a person invests capital into a business, they are putting those financial resources at risk. If the business fails, the capital may be only partially recovered and could be completely lost. That's the risk people take in investing.

However, if the business succeeds, those who have risked their capital are rewarded with profits from the operations of the business. This is why free enterprise is also called capitalism. There is nothing immoral or unethical about capitalism, as long as all agreements are honestly and freely made.

However, the banking fraud discussed in the last chapter is an immoral aspect of our current capitalism because it involves manipulation of the money system, giving some people an unfair advantage over others. The other two parts of our current form of capitalism that I consider to be immoral have to do with the definition of property. I discussed this briefly in my review of our unalienable rights but will expand upon it in this chapter.

We Are Stewards, Not Owners of the Earth

There is a difference between possession and ownership of property. We may be in possession of something that is not our property. Previously, I suggested that the only way we can create property is when some aspect of our creativity and capital is added to something. We cannot own what we had no hand in creating. Since we did not create the earth we live on, the air we breathe, or the water we drink, we cannot call it our property. Scripture would suggest that what God made is God's property.

> The earth is the LORD'S, and the fulness thereof; the world, and they that dwell therein. (Psalm 24:1, KJV)

Thus, we have stewardship, but not ownership, over the earth's resources. A steward is someone who is allowed to manage someone else's property. Many Native American tribes recognized this fact. For example, Chief Crazy Horse said, "One does not sell the earth upon which the people walk."[48] Chief Joseph states it this way, "The earth is the mother of all people, and all people should have equal rights upon

---

[48] As quoted in Bury My Heart at Wounded Knee (1970) by Dee Brown, Ch. 12 (https://en.wikiquote.org/wiki/Crazy_Horse)

it."[49] Here is one more example from Chief Seattle, when the United States government was pressuring him to sell two million acres.

> How can you buy or sell the sky, the warmth of the land? The idea is strange to us. If we do not own the freshness of the air and sparkle of the water, how can you buy them?[50]

Again, my point is that the resources of the earth do not become our property until we add our own labor to them. Until then, they are the common stewardship of all mankind, who were commanded in the beginning to "multiply and replenish the earth" (Gen. 1:28, KJV). Replenish means that we are not supposed to just take from the earth; we are also supposed to give back to the earth and make certain that what we receive is replenished. In other words, we are to be stewards over God's resources and make sure they are properly cared for.

Stewardship versus Real Estate

In the Old Testament, families received lands for their inheritance that were divided by lot. Here in Utah where I live, as the pioneers came to the various valleys and laid out plots of land for the creation of cities and towns, the various lots were also divided by lot. This means that a reference to each piece of land was put onto a paper, which was put into the "hat" or lottery. The head of each family group drew one of the slips of paper to find out which piece of property was to be their lot in the town.

Under this Old Testament system, people possessed the land but they did not own it. The land was received as a stewardship. As a family worked the land, planting crops, building a home and other structures,

---

[49] Lincoln Hall Speech in Washington D.C., January 14, 1879. (https://www.azquotes.com/quote/546707)

[50] https://www.csun.edu/~vcpsy00h/seattle.htm

they acquired property through the improvements made on the land. They owned these improvements, but not the land itself.

Since people need space to live, the right to life suggests that all human beings have a right to occupy land. They have the natural right to possess (or occupy) a piece of the land God created. This is different from the notion of real estate, however.

Real estate comes from the idea of the royal estate under feudal serfdom. In this system, the king or nobleman was said to own the land, not just the improvements on it, and the subjects who lived on the land were renters on the estate, subject to taxation on a portion of all they produced. This means that people did not have the right to fully own what they created.

Although acquiring real estate is a popular way of amassing personal wealth, there's a problem with it. There's an often-overlooked passage in Isaiah, which alludes to this problem.

> Woe unto them that join house to house, that lay field
> to field, till there be no place, that they may be placed
> alone in the midst of the earth! (Isa. 5:8, KJV)

The business of real estate is one of buying up property and the improvements thereon, adding house to house and field to field, as Isaiah said, and then being able to profit by forcing others to pay rent in order to have a place to live. What happens if a few wealthy people gradually buy up all the homes in the community so that everyone living there has to pay rent to them in order to have a place to live? Such a practice always allows those who have greater wealth to use it to enrich themselves, usually at the expense of the poor.

The property tax charged by government is also part of this corrupt system, since a person can lose his/her right to possess the land and own the improvements thereon if he/she fails to pay the annual "rent" to the government. This ability to expel people from the land and force them to live on land owned by others denies people part of their basic God-given right to live. The government also does this by locking up unoccupied land, thus denying ordinary people access to the land and resources God created.

Denying those who have become homeless a place to live is an immoral act, since a person has an unalienable right to occupy some place on the earth. A society that provides no place for the poor and homeless to live without paying rent to someone is not a moral society.

The Evils of Usury

The other practice which enables the wealthy to take advantage of the poor was alluded to in the last chapter. It is the practice of usury or charging interest on monetary loans. Although this practice is also deeply embedded in our capitalistic culture, it is clearly condemned in the Old Testament common law system.

> You shall not charge interest (usury) on loans to your brother, interest on money, interest on food, interest on anything that is lent for interest. You may charge a foreigner interest, but you may not charge your brother interest, that the Lord your God may bless you in all that you undertake in the land that you are entering to take possession of it. (Deut. 23:19–20, ESV)

> If you loan money to my people, to the poor among you, don't be like a creditor to them and don't impose interest on them. (Ex. 22:25, NAS)

Although some people have argued that this only has reference to personal loans made to friends and neighbors and does not apply to commercial loans, I don't believe this is true. In fact, I believe that allowing this practice is one of the pitfalls of society and a primary way that the rich take advantage of the poor.

> The wealthy rule over the poor, and anyone who borrows is a slave to the lender. (Prov. 22:7, ISV)

Interest is a Rent Charged on Money

The term usury refers to a fee one pays for the temporary use of another person's property. It's synonymous with the concept of rent. If I own a home or a car and agree to rent the property to you for a period of time, there's nothing wrong with this. After all, property is subject to wear and tear, which causes it to lose value without upkeep and maintenance. Therefore, it's appropriate to pay a use fee for using the property, hence the term *use-ury*.

Interest is a rent payment on money. When I loan someone money with interest, I'm charging a usage fee for the other person to be able to use my money. The above biblical passages suggest that we shouldn't be charging people, at least not those in our own country, a use fee for borrowing money.

To explain why allowing people to charge interest on loans isn't a good practice, let's start by remembering that money is the medium of exchange. Its purpose is to make it easier to trade for goods and services. If we allow the medium of exchange to become a commodity itself, instead of being used to facilitate the exchange of goods and services, it ultimately leads to wealth being concentrated in the hands of a few.

With that understanding, I want to return to the hypothetical community of 100 people I referred to in chapter seven. Let's suppose that each of these 100 people all start off with an equal amount of coins, one thousand dollars in gold. Each also produces goods and services for the benefit of other members of the community, which causes these coins to circulate through the community as good and services are traded.

As is going to always happen, some people work harder or create goods and services on which people place more value. These people will naturally receive a larger amount of the coins than others. As long as these people are using the money to purchase the goods and services of others in the community, however, the money will circulate and everyone will benefit from that circulation.

However, what happens if a wealthier person decides to rent out his or her excess coins instead of using them to purchase goods and services? The person who borrows the coins, who is likely to be one of the poorer members of the community, will use them to pay for goods and services, but they also have to return the borrowed money with interest.

This means that they have to come up with even more money than they got from the loan to pay the lender. The lender now has even more gold coins to lend, which means they continually acquire a larger and larger percentage of the coins in circulation.

One can readily see that the supply of coins in circulation is going to gradually shrink as more and more of the coins wind up in the hands of the lenders, while fewer coins wind up in the hands of the borrowers. This would happen even if the money was never devalued and allows those who are wealthy to increase their wealth at the expense of those who have less money.

So, it makes sense to me that the medium of exchange should not become a commodity to be rented. One reason for this is that when there is an honest money system, the money has a fixed value. It is not subject to wear and tear through use the way a house, a car, or a horse would be. When returned, the lender should be able to purchase the same amount of goods and services he could have before the loan was given. He has lost nothing as long as the loan is repaid.

This is different than investing money into a business. I've already pointed out that this places the money at risk. The business isn't paying back the medium of exchange; it is paying back profits if the business is successful.

This could even be done by banks, provided that the bank didn't pretend your money was still there. Instead of an "on demand" note, you might be required to leave your money in the bank for one, five, or ten years and be promised a share of the profits (or losses) from the bank's investments into businesses.

Jubilee and the Forgiveness of Debts

The Old Testament had a unique solution to the two problems I've described above. Besides the prohibition on lending money with interest, the Old Testament also protected the rights of people who couldn't pay their debts or temporarily lost the lands of their inheritance for one reason or another. It did this via the land Sabbaths and the Jubilee Year.

Land Sabbaths were similar to the idea of the Sabbath day, one day set aside each week for rest and worship, except that the land Sabbaths were one year set aside out of every seven. During the Sabbath year, farmers were to allow their land to rest. If modern farmers were to allow the land to rest in this manner every seven years, there would be less depletion of the soil, but that is not the focus of our discussion. What we're interested in is the fact that all debts incurred during the previous six years were to be forgiven during the Sabbath year.

> At the end of every seven years you shall grant a relief of debts. And this is the manner of the release: Every creditor that has lent anything unto his neighbor shall release it; he shall not require it of his neighbor, or of his brother, because it is called the LORD'S release." (Deut. 15:1-2, NKJV)

Thus, under Old Testament law, debts were supposed to be forgiven and wiped clean every seven years. This would prohibit people from using loans to consolidate the wealth of the land at the expense of the poor.

The Founding Fathers did recognize the need for people to escape from excessive debt by authorizing federal bankruptcy laws in the Constitution. I believe this is a righteous principle and can be a modern application of this principle of debt forgiveness.

The Jubilee and Real Estate

After seven cycles of these sabbatical years (7x7 or 49 years), the fiftieth year was to be a year of jubilee. During the Jubilee year, the land was also to rest from cultivation but instead of debts being forgiven, all land that had been mortgaged or lost by the poor was to be returned to its original owners. In other words, people had the right to reclaim family lands.

> And you shall consecrate the fiftieth year, and pro-
> claim liberty throughout the land to all its inhabitants.
> It shall be a jubilee for you, when each of you shall
> return to his property and each of you shall return to
> his clan. That fiftieth year shall be a jubilee for you; in
> it you shall neither sow nor reap what grows of itself
> nor gather the grapes from the undressed vines. For
> it is a jubilee. It shall be holy to you. You may eat
> the produce of the field.In this year of jubilee each of
> you shall return to his property. (Lev. 25:10-13 ESV)

Notice that the Jubilee is a year to "proclaim liberty" and that part of this liberty is restoring lands a family had lost through poverty or debt so they could again have inherited the land and have a place to live. Here is another passage about this returning of the land to the people.

The land, moreover, shall not be sold permanently, for
the land is Mine; for you are but aliens and sojourners
with Me. Thus for every piece of your property, you
are to provide for the redemption of the land. (Lev.
25:23-24, KJV)

Notice that land that was an inheritance could not be permanently
sold because the land is God's property, not man's property, and he
desires that everyone have a right to inherit the land. Thus, the Jubilee
prevented the accumulation of real estate and allowed everyone to possess a portion of land without paying rent to others.

We Need a Jubilee

As our nation becomes increasingly enslaved to debt, we are losing our
freedom. Not only are we trading notes of debt as if they were money,
people are constantly having to borrow through credit cards, mort-
gages, and other loans to be able to live. As I write this, the government is over 28 trillion dollars in debt. If you add up the liabilities for
future social security, Medicare, retirement pensions, and other promised obligations, the total debt jumps to 82 trillion. This does not count
the debt owed by states and local governments.

Even though there are 330 million people in America, only about
125 million are taxpayers. The federal debt alone means that every citizen, man, woman and child, is currently obligated for $84,000 in fed-
eral debt. If you look at the taxpayers only, this is about $222,000 per
taxpayer. With the medium income of $35,000 per taxpayer, every
taxpayer would have to work for many years for free to pay this debt.
This cannot be sustained, let alone allowed to increase by adding more
and more government spending.

Perhaps we need a year of Jubilee where we wipe the slate clean by
forgiving all debts and allowing people to retain their homes, cars, and
other personal possessions. There would be nothing immoral about

such an action, since the money said to be owed was fraudulent and unconstitutional to begin with. Of course, it would take a widespread change in people's attitudes about money and property for a Jubilee year to be accepted.

As for the problem of real estate, the government originally made lands available through purchase or homesteading. Now, however, the government claims ownership of much of the property in the United States, especially in the West where a large portion of the land is under the management of the BLM (Bureau of Land Management) or other government agencies. Homeless people are forbidden from living on this government land, which could be used to give poor or homeless people a place to live.

There are also many abandoned properties around the country. The improvements on this land are deteriorating from lack of care, but the land is locked up by those who claim ownership. If a person isn't making use of the land, could it be released to those who need a place to live if they will start caring for it?

These are all questions I have pondered, but none of this will be possible until people wake up to the need for an honest money system and an end to fraudulent banking practices, usury, and concepts of real estate. That's why I stress that it is the moral character of the people of a nation that makes a society truly free and not the government or the current capitalistic system. So, the ultimate solution to these problems lies in changing our attitudes about money and economics, as I discuss in the next chapter.

CHAPTER FIFTEEN

THE ROOT OF
ALL EVIL

I was raised in a lower middle-class family. My father worked two jobs to support us and although we always had a home, clothing, food, and other necessities of life, we didn't have any luxuries. That fact, coupled with a standard public education, made me extremely financially illiterate.

Like many people who struggle to make ends meet, you can easily buy into the idea that money is evil and people who have too much money are greedy and self-centered. That covetous spirit, which violates the tenth Commandment, prevents a person from really understanding what money is and how money works.

It took me a long time to unlearn what I thought I knew about money. But once I did, I realized that the Scripture is right when it says, "the *love* of money is the root of all evil" (1 Tim. 6:10 KJV). Money itself is not good or evil. It's simply a tool for trade. It is when your heart gets set upon money that the desire for money acts within you for evil.

As motivational author and teacher Bob Proctor says, many people love money and use people. Instead, he suggests, we need to love people and use money.[51]

Jesus put it this way:

---

[51] Bob Proctor, Instagram Post by Bob Proctor, May 12, 2016, https://www.pinterest.com/pin/569142471642136903/

No man can serve two masters: for either he will hate the one, and love the other; or else he will hold to the one, and despise the other. Ye cannot serve God and mammon. (Mat. 6:24, KJV)

It's interesting that He didn't say you can't serve God and the devil. He said you can't serve God and mammon; mammon being defined as riches or wealth. If we put the desire for riches and wealth ahead of loving our neighbor as ourselves, then we're falling prey to the temptation to break the common law and trespass against our neighbor, either directly or indirectly, by assigning that task to our agent, the government.

There is nothing morally wrong with profit, as long as it is done through honest and free trade, but we need to make money our servant, not our master. This needs to happen to us as individuals, but it also needs to happen on a national level if a country is to be free and prosperous. So, in this chapter, I hope to share some of the information I learned that made me finally become financially literate, which also has improved my own personal financial situation.

Production and Prosperity

Realizing how financially illiterate most people are, Robert Kiosaki wrote a series of books starting with "Rich Dad, Poor Dad." His books were designed to educate people about how money works. He says that most people think that having more money will solve their money problems, but this simply isn't true. As soon as the average person gets some extra money, they immediately spend it. We might say they "consume" the extra money.[52]

That's because, as I've already suggested, money is only the medium of exchange, not the ultimate thing we desire. Money is only the tool

---

[52] Robert Kiyosaki, "More money doesn't solve problems," March 8, 2013, https://kiyosaki-blog.blogspot.com/2013/03/robert-kiyosaki-more-money-doesnt-solve.html

that enables us to trade the fruits of our labor (our property) for the fruits of someone else's labor (their property). In order to have something to trade, we first have to produce something that other people value. That is, we need to shift the attitude we have as a consumer and adopt the attitude of a producer.

Producers are people who think about the wants and needs of others and find ways to labor productively to supply what other people want and need. People readily give their money to producers because the producer is laboring to create what the consumer perceives as valuable.

When we've produced value for other people and have received money in return, we can be consumers. Consuming is a self-centered activity that focuses on what I want, which is to get as much value as I possibly can for my labor and money. To put it succinctly, a productive person earns the money, while a consumer spends the money.

Money and the Law of the Harvest

When I complained about our family's lack of money as a teenager, my mother used to tell me, "Poor people have poor ways." I thought that she was being very judgmental about people's misfortune, but years later I started to understand what that really meant. While people do suffer from circumstances that cause them financial problems, there is a difference between someone struggling financially and someone being stuck in a poverty mentality.

My awakening about money began when I started to understand how the Law of the Harvest applies to money. If it is true that we reap what we sow, then the average person primarily has a consumer mindset when it comes to money. That means they want to get as much as possible, while giving as little as possible. In our consumer mindset, we're always hunting for bargains and "free" is especially attractive because it suggests we can get something of value without having to give something of value.

What I realized was this: If I'm always trying to get stuff from other people and avoiding having to give other people very much, then the Law of the Harvest will return the same energy to me. I will get as little as possible in exchange for my efforts. In other words, I'll earn very little money for the effort I put forth.

I realized that this was what a poverty mindset really is—it was sowing the energy of trying to get a lot for a little, thus reaping a crop of getting a little for a lot. I realized that if I wanted to prosper, I had to be reverse this. I had to be willing to be generous, to give more than was required.

The Christian motivational speaker and author Zig Ziglar was fond of saying it this way: "You can get anything you want in this life, if you'll only help enough other people get what they want."[53] The author of the famous book, *Think and Grow Rich*, Napoleon Hill also stressed this idea, using the biblical idea of "going the extra mile." He said that you should always render more service than you're getting paid to render, which means that you'd eventually receive more in return. In other words, when laboring to *earn* money, give more than you receive.[54] Hill put it this way, "Render more and better service that that for which you are paid, and sooner or later you will receive compound interest upon compound interest on your investment."[55]

Ralph Waldo Emerson's essay on Compensation stresses this idea as well.

> Men suffer all their life long, under the foolish super-
> stition that they can be cheated. But it is as impossible

[53] Zig Ziglar, Secrets of Closing the Sale (1982). (https://www.azquotes.com/quote/1465083)

[54] Robert Newel, Going the Extra Mile, The Napoleon Hill Foundation, https://www.naphill.org/focus-instructors/going-the-extra-mile/

[55] Sid Shaw, Going the Extra Mile: The Classic Success Principle, The Napoleon Hill Foundation, https://www.naphill.org/focus-instructors/going-the-extra-mile-the-classic/

for a man to be cheated by anyone but himself, as for a thing to be and not to be at the same time. There is a third silent party to all our bargains. The nature and soul of things takes on itself the guaranty of the fulfillment of every contract, so that honest service cannot come to loss. If you serve an ungrateful master, serve him the more. Put God in your debt. Every stroke shall be repaid. The longer the payment is [withheld], the better for you; for compound interest on compound interest is the rate and usage of this [exchanger]."[56]

Trusting God Instead of Man

Practicing land Sabbaths and Jubilee years by generously releasing debts and restoring property, as well as forgoing cultivating the land, was an act of faith in God. It forces one to trust in the idea expressed by Emerson that God acknowledges and rewards those who generously give of themselves and that one cannot get real gain by cheating or being selfish.

The simple truth is this—in the absence of government monopolies and regulatory practices, it is the person who gives the greatest value for the lowest price who succeeds. By constantly evaluating how they can provide for others at the lowest possible price, they receive a Law of the Harvest compensation for their efforts, but the harvest often comes long after the crop was sown.

In my own life, I started putting these practices into action in the late 1980s and my income tripled in just a few years. I also started my business as a part-time effort in May of 1986, while working at a full-time corporate job. For three and a half years I didn't spend one dime of the money the business made; I put it back into growing the business.

---

[56] Emerson, *Essays – First Series*, p 83

When I quit my corporate job and started on my own in January of 1990, I still made most of my earnings for the next two years teaching classes for the same company. It wasn't until 1992, five and a half years after I started it, that my business was able to provide a full-time income for me. In other words, I had to sow a lot before I began to receive the harvest back from what I had sowed.

Over the years, various people who claimed to be "great at business" would tell me I wasn't charging enough or I should cut corners on cost. I observed that such things never work in the long run and many of these people who were supposed to be "great at business" never prospered at it the way I did.

The Law of the Harvest can't be circumvented. If you receive something without giving something in return, the law will see that you will later have to give something without receiving anything in return. On the other hand, if you give without receiving anything in return, the Law of the Harvest will bring you something in the future for which you don't have to give anything.

So, what does all this have to do with government? Simple. It explains why government welfare programs increase poverty.

Poverty and the Welfare State

Many people today believe that people can be lifted out of poverty if we simply raise the minimum wage or supply everyone with a guaranteed income. In other words, they equate money with prosperity, not the goods and services money is used to purchase. These ideas may sound good in theory, but they don't work in the real world. The belief that constantly giving people money or favors they haven't earned will make those people's lives better arises from the financial illiteracy I alluded to at the beginning of the chapter.

To understand this, let's take an absurd position. Let's suppose that everyone has money, but no one is working to produce any goods or services. Would people be wealthy if no one was growing food, building homes, making clothing, and so forth? Of course not; that's absurd! Money won't feed, clothe, or house anyone unless it can be traded for these necessities, and someone has to work to produce them before they can be sold.

Now, let's reverse that. Let's suppose that everyone in a society is producing goods and services and nobody is idle. Let's also suppose that money is in short supply. Will people be prosperous then? Of course, they will. You can trade goods and services without money; money just makes it easier. It is the abundance of goods and services that are the basis of real wealth.

Having looked at both ends of the spectrum, let's suppose that 20 percent of the population stops producing goods and services, but there is more money available. Does this mean that everyone will be wealthier? No, because about 20 percent of the population isn't producing real wealth.

If we take some money from the people who are productive and give it to those who are not, does this increase the supply of goods and services? No, because the people getting the welfare benefits are only consuming, not producing. If you think about this, the larger the percentage of the people who are consuming, but not producing, the less real wealth there is. Plus, the money is always flowing from the consumers to the producers, which means the producers will always receive more than the consumers.

If we add this to the fact that the Law of the Harvest suggests that if we are getting something without having sowed our productivity first, then we are going to be constantly receiving less for our efforts. Anyone who attempts to reap what they have not sown still has to pay the price. They are in debt to the universe, and the debt will be repaid. Our high national debt illustrates the truth behind this principle—at some point it will no longer be sustainable.

The Law of the Harvest explains why socialism never works in practice. Again, and again, the implementation of socialist policies brings a nation to poverty. Taking what is not your property by the force of government causes the same energy to return to you. Just because you took what was not yours through the instrument of government does not remove the moral repercussions of this action. As people reap without sowing, they will soon be forced to sow without reaping.

My wife lived in Ukraine when it was part of the USSR and she has personally told me about people having money, but there was nothing to buy with it. She also told me how everyone was jealous of the success of others and instead of building them up, they were always wanting to bring them down to their level.

That's why a free market economy is the only system that can help lift people out of poverty. It encourages productivity, which means it encourages the production of property. If I have to work to create value for others in order to get money, then more property is available for others to consume, which also means there is more real wealth. Of course, that works best when there is an honest money system that is not based on debt and usury.

You Can't Be Independent by Being Dependent

Have you ever seen a spoiled child? Parents who continuously indulge their children by giving them whatever they want and requiring little in return keep children in a state of dependency. Being dependent means that someone else has to provide you with the things you want and need. You are not able to obtain these things for yourself.

In contrast, being independent means that one has the knowledge, skills, and motivation to take care of their own needs and wants. Independent people are free people, which is why freedom is also known as independence. Dependent people are not free because they are forever subject to those on whom they depend.

Children who are spoiled are not prepared to face the real world, where it takes work and effort to make things happen. A similar thing happens in society when government hands out "free stuff." People begin to feel entitled, which means that they somehow feel they should be able to receive without first having to give. A country where a large percentage of people think this way will wind up being a poor country because there will be little produced in the way of goods and services.

As I learned to be generous, I also learned another valuable lesson, which is—giving too much to other people doesn't help them. That's because money that isn't earned by our own productivity can actually be a curse because of the operation of the Law of the Harvest. For example, many people who win the lottery wind up financially worse off in the long run. Children of parents who are rich often wind up poor. I personally knew a couple whose wife inherited three million dollars. It was nearly all gone in just a couple of years.

In contrast, a society of people who recognize the value of work and understand the principle that you "can't get something for nothing" will be a prosperous country because the more people there are who are being productive, the greater the wealth of the nation. The illusion people need to break free of is that money creates wealth. Money is only a tool for trading real wealth; it is people's creative labor produces real wealth. Desiring money, without having to provide something of value to others, is desiring to get something without giving anything in return. It violates the Law of the Harvest and will eventually reap the crop of poverty.

You do not need to wait for society to change to implement what I have explained in this chapter. You can start today. It's just one way you have of using your social power to change society. I'll explain what I mean by social power in the next chapter.

Chapter Sixteen

Social Power

When I was in eighth grade, our teacher asked us to write two essays: one about our "real" self, and the other about our "ideal" self. I got marked down because the essay I wrote about my "ideal" self began by saying that I saw myself as a leader in an ideal society. I spent the bulk of this essay talking about this ideal society and not about the ideal me. The truth was that I couldn't picture an ideal me without picturing a larger, ideal world.

There was a grave error in my youthful thinking, however. I assumed that an ideal government could create an ideal world. Since then, I've learned that it can't. Government exists because people trespass against each other, failing to uphold the Golden Rule in their lives. The more immoral the people, the more powerful and immoral the government will become, but only up to a point. At some point, the people become so immoral that the society collapses and chaos reigns until a new government emerges.

The reverse is also true. The more moral a people become, the less government they need. If there is very little crime, there is no need for a large police force. If people can peacefully settle their own disputes, there is no need for government courts to settle the disputes for them through civil law. If people love and respect each other and help each other out in time of need, then there is also no need for a welfare state.

Over time, I came to understand that seeking political power was not the best way to fix society, as there is a limit to what one can achieve by force. The imagined "dictator of the world" scenario, put forth in chapter one, is not a likely possibility unless you had widespread support among the people for your leadership. A leader who stands in moral opposition to the vast majority of the citizens will be thrust from power by some type of revolution. An immoral people will oust a good leader, and a moral people will rid themselves of a corrupt leader.

Government is Not the Only Source of Power

Many people see government as the primary and, perhaps, only means for improving the world. While Mao may be right that *political* power grows out of the barrel of a gun, there are other sources of power that have a strong influence on the world. These include family, religion, entertainment, education, and culture.

In 1850, the French philosopher Fredric Bastiat wrote a book titled *The Law*. It is one of the best discourses on freedom and natural law ever written. In it, he states:

> Socialism, like the ancient ideas from which it springs, confuses the distinction between government and society. As a result of this, every time we object to a thing being done by government, the socialists conclude that we object to its being done at all. We disapprove of state education. Then the socialists say that we are opposed to any education. We object to a state religion. Then the socialists say that we want no religion at all. We object to a state-enforced equality. Then they say that we are against equality. And so on, and so on. It is as if the socialists were to accuse us of not wanting persons to eat because we do not want the state to raise grain.[57]

---

[57] Frederic Bastiat, *The Law* (Foundation for Economic Education: Irvington-on-Hudson, NY), p 32-33

As Bastiat points out, government is not the only way to get things done, and in most cases, is not even the best way to get things done. I sum up my own opinion about government's efficiency when I've told people, "If you want to get something done in the most costly and inefficient way possible, assign it to government."

Government power is limited because it relies primarily on fear. People comply with government out of the fear of what will happen to them if they don't. However, there are forces that are more powerful than fear. One of these forces is the desire to be free, to control our own lives. Another is the desire to get along with others, to "love and be loved."

Many people have risen above their fear and courageously given up their property and their lives to defend the cause of liberty. To feel like they belong, most people voluntarily give up some of their independence and conform to social norms. Thus, force and the threat of violence are actually less powerful than courage and love.

Remember the thought experiment in chapter one that put you into power as the dictator of the world? You wouldn't have to use force alone to influence people. In fact, for many issues, it wouldn't be the most effective way to make the changes you desire in the world. Leadership that involves teaching, persuading, and encouraging people to voluntarily co-operate would work better in many cases. And, you don't have to have political power to start exercising leadership to influence society.

The Family as a Model for Society

Let me explain why it's important to balance force (or violence) with more voluntary forms of influence using families as an example. I've watched families for many years to try to understand what works and doesn't work in parenting. My observations, and my study of books on successful parenting, have led me to the conclusion that healthy families are those that successfully balance the two forces of love and discipline. Unhealthy families tend to gravitate to one pole or the other.

On the one hand, you see the parents whose primary focus is discipline. They exercise a kind of dictatorial control over their children. These parents often shout, yell, call their children names, threaten them with violence (spanking or worse), and then carry out that violence in an attempt to control their children. When I observed families like this, I noted that even if the children seem well-behaved on the surface, they are often secretly rebellious. They may also wind up being abusive to others as adults or become adults with a victim mentality that leaves them crushed in spirit. But the primary weakness in these families is the general lack of family unity and cohesiveness. There is an unwillingness to voluntarily do good, as I defined earlier. Family members are generally unwilling to voluntarily make sacrifices to help other family members.

Some family cultures go to the opposite extreme. On this end, parents don't correct or guide their children very much at all. Instead, they shower their children with love, try to protect them from every hardship of life, and are constantly trying to give their children whatever they want. In effect, they try to bribe their children into being loving and good. Parents like this are afraid to correct their children, even when they are badly misbehaving. Children raised in families like this are often self-centered and selfish, having unreasonable expectations of what others "should" do for them. They are also unwilling to make sacrifices for others and thus cannot do real good in the world.

The most successful families I've seen use loving but firm restraints. They set boundaries for their children but also allow them choices. They discipline their children but also show them love and kindness while giving that discipline. These families manage to find a healthy balance between the poles of indulgence and domination. In my observation, they tend to produce children who can exercise self-restraint but can also do good by making voluntary sacrifices for the benefit of others.

In society, these two poles are represented by the extremes of conservatism and liberalism. One is a controlling or ruling spirit that wants to maintain order and disciple without kindness and mercy, while the other is a free spirit that makes excuses for criminal behavior and thinks that if we generously took care of everyone through the government, everybody would be good. Neither of these extremes will create a free and prosperous society. Instead, we need to find the proper balance between these poles.

The Force of Culture

Like a family, a country has to determine when the force of the government is justified and when it is not. The zero aggression principle,[58] also known as the non-aggression principle,[59] is that force should only be used to counteract those who use force to violate the rights of others. All other problems can be solved through the forces that shape culture, such as entertainment, education, family and ethnic ties, and religion.

Oddly enough, the people who have sought to undermine the American republic have understood the power of culture in shaping society. They have used the entertainment industry, government-controlled education, the breakdown of family ties, and the promotion of atheism to create cultural force to shift the government away from the principles laid down in the Declaration of Independence and the Constitution.

If we wish to counteract what is happening, we need to use more than our vote to change it. We need to start working with culture. We need to educate people about the moral basis of liberty. We need to create entertainment that promotes good and sound moral principles. We need to strengthen families and voluntary organizations like churches. We need to push for less government power and more social

---

[58] What is the Zero Aggression Principle (ZAP), https://zeroaggressionproject.org/mental-lever/zero-aggression-principle/

[59] Non-Aggression Principle, https://www.libertarianism.org/topics/non-aggression-principle

power. A good start is to try to solve our problems through voluntary cooperation with others instead of through government.

My observation is that when a society, like a family, overuses force as a means of achieving social ends, it doesn't result in a culture of co-operation and mutual respect. Instead, it produces citizens who become less and less co-operative with each other. Instead of trying to work out their differences and find mutually beneficial solutions, it increases the tendency toward power struggles, fostering an "us" versus "them" mentality.

To illustrate what can happen when the government lets go of an area of social responsibility, let's look at a practical example of something people used to believe was a necessary job of government—religion.

Prior to the American constitutional system, European countries had strong ties between church and state. Taxes were often used to support the church because it was believed that the church created a moral fabric in society, and without it, civilization could not endure. Many of the colonies followed this example and had state-supported churches. However, these states were concerned that the new federal government would support one church over another. To prevent this, freedom of religion was placed into the American Bill of Rights, and governments stopped financially supporting churches.

As the state stopped supporting religion, religion didn't die off. In fact, it actually did the opposite; it flourished. During the early 1800s, Americans developed a great deal of religious fervor, and churches actually grew, all through voluntary contributions, not state taxes. When there is a social need for something, people will find ways to satisfy that need without government force.

Taking Responsibility and Restoring Liberty

In his popular book *Twelve Rules for Life*, the sixth rule psychologist Jordan Peterson advocates is that people set their own houses in order before trying to change the world.[60] This is sound advice. All too often we act as armchair philosophers, thinking that our ideas are good ones and should be forced on the world through politics.

However, I often look at people who do this and find the words of Jonathan Edward's song *Sunshine Go Away Today* running through my mind, "He can't even run his own life, I'll be damned if he'll run mine."[61] I actually think this of myself. Returning to our thought experiment in chapter one, I know I'm not smart enough to run the whole world. I think power needs to be spread out, something the Founding Fathers understood when they separated political power both horizontally through the three branches of government and vertically through the system of county, state, and federal governments.

I have long recognized the wisdom of the Founding Fathers in creating this vertical separation of powers. Anything which can be left to an individual's personal discretion should be. Anything which can be managed at a local level should be. What needs to be managed at a state level should be. Very little needs to be managed at the federal level of government. The people closest to any situation are more likely to come up with a good answer to a problem than strangers living thousands of miles away.

Personal Responsibility

So one of the most important steps to advancing the cause of freedom is to stop handing over more responsibilities to the government and instead take more responsibility over our own lives. Years ago, I read an essay about responsibility that has stuck with me ever since. I've lost the original, so I don't know the author, but he spoke of a situation I was very familiar with as a young father. A baby wakes up crying in the middle of the night. The baby wakes up the husband, whose first

---

[60] Jordan B. Peterson, Twelve Rules for Life (Toronto: Random House Canada, 2018), pp. 147-149

[61] http://www.songlyrics.com/jonathan-edwards/sunshine-go-away-today-lyrics/

thought is, *Maybe I should get the baby this time and give my wife a break.* After all, the thought occurs to him, *She's gotten up with the baby twice and she seems so tired, maybe I should take a turn.*

However, instead of obeying this first impulse to do good, he thinks, *But I have to work tomorrow, and she doesn't. She can take a nap during the day, and I can't. It's her responsibility, why should I have to do it?* Then he starts feeling angry and annoyed.

The author pointed out that his first impulse, which was based in being helpful and considerate, was a good one. He recognized a problem and felt prompted to do something about it. However, he failed to heed that prompting, and when he started rationalizing, he started getting angry with his wife.

This is what we tend to do. Instead of taking personal responsibility and trying to figure out how we can be of help in a situation, we often rationalize why we can't help. We're not powerful; we don't have enough money; we don't have the time, and so forth. And, because we aren't heeding our own inner impulse to do good, we start looking for someone else to blame for the problem so we can push the responsibility off onto others.

I believe this is exactly what we're doing when we want to make the government fix all the cultural problems we see. We get to "virtue signal" how good we are by supporting government leaders who claim they'll fix our problems when, in reality, we are not really doing anything worthwhile personally. We need to change that. It's what I did. I've applied all the principles I discuss in this book into my private life in dealing with people close to me. It was only after proving they work on that level that I decided to write this book and advocate them on a larger scale.

Government and the Will of the People

I began this book by laying out the premise that government power is force. It is the power to use guns and violence against people who fail to comply with government rules. I also proposed that we need to question ourselves about what the moral use of force and violence is. Instead of asking if a government policy being advocated is "good for us," we should ask, "Is this a moral application for the use of force or the threat of force?"

I'm pleading with you to recognize that you can't create a better world through the use of government force. All you can morally do through that agent is restrain evil. A good society will only come as the individuals within that society seek to live by correct moral principles. If the majority of people become immoral, no government power will be able to prevent society from becoming corrupt.

There's a quote attributed to the French aristocrat Alexis de Tocqueville who wrote *Democracy in America* after touring the country in 1830-1831. Although it's questionable if he actually said it, it has often been repeated and still illustrates an important principle.

> America is great because she is good, and if America ever ceases to be good, she will cease to be great.[62]

Whatever the origins of this quote, it speaks truth. It was also reflected in the farewell address of our first president, George Washington, when he said:

> It is substantially true that virtue or morality is a necessary spring of popular government. The rule, indeed, extends with more or less force to every species of free government.[63]

---

[62] See https://faithandamericanhistory.wordpress.com/2016/07/27/america-is-great-because-america-is-good-part-one/

[63] https://billofrightsinstitute.org/primary-sources/washingtons-farewell-address

He also maintained that religion and morality were the "... dispositions and habits which lead to political prosperity," and that we should use caution in indulging the supposition that "morality can be maintained without religion." He also stated that "reason and experience both forbid us to expect that national morality can prevail in exclusion of religious principle."

What makes a country great is not its wealth or military might, but its moral integrity. As people lose their moral compass, the Law of the Harvest will remove their wealth and political power. For that reason, I've felt a little uncomfortable with the slogan, "Make America Great," as it sounds like we should be pursuing power and the pride that goes with it. I think we should adopt the slogan, "Make America Good." The more we can collectively return to sound moral principles, the more we will naturally become great.

Morally Evaluating Our Support of Government

I suggest that you ponder the principles I've discussed in this book and how they apply to your personal and political life. Throughout this book, I've stressed the idea of the Law of the Harvest as an immutable law that always operates on each of us. We cannot trespass against the rights of others, either in our personal lives or in our social, business, or political lives without reaping the crop we sow.

Many people rooted in biblical principles are concerned about the moral decline in America and the judgments it may bring upon our nation. As many have recognized, the situation can be turned around if those who have faith in God will repent and pray for God's blessings, as recorded in 2 Chron. 7:14.

> If my people, which are called by my name, shall
> humble themselves, and pray, and seek my face,
> and turn from their wicked ways; then will I hear

from heaven, and will forgive their sin, and will heal
their land.

Our faith and prayers can make a difference but only if they are
coupled with repentance. In my experience, most Christians focus on
issues like drugs, legal abortion, and sexual immorality as areas where
the nation needs repentance. However, I don't think God will heal
our land if we don't also repent for using the government as a means
to tread upon the rights of others, especially in supporting the government committing theft and murder.

Remember that we delegate our authority to the government
when we vote and give our verbal consent to government policies. If
we ask the government to do things for us that we know would be
crimes if we did them ourselves, then we are asking the government
to commit crimes on our behalf. We are participating in what Bastiat
called "legal plunder."

> But how is this legal plunder to be identified? Quite
> simply. See if the law takes from some persons what
> belongs to them and gives it to other persons to whom
> it does not belong. See if the law benefits one citizen
> at the expense of another by doing what the citizen
> himself cannot do without committing a crime.[64]

When we support the government in trespassing against the life,
liberty, or property of others for personal gain or the gain of others that
we support, we are participants in the act. Therefore, the moral repercussions of the Law of the Harvest will come back on us, and not just
our agents in the government. Realizing this made a dramatic change
in my thoughts about what is proper and improper for the government

---

[64] Bastiat, The Law, p 21

to do and made me very cautious about supporting the "lesser of two evils" in the political spectrum.

Believers in biblical principles of common law need to repent of this. Personally, I adopted the following standard for deciding what is appropriate or inappropriate for the government to do; I ask myself this question, "Would I be willing to use a gun to force my friends, neighbors, and, most importantly, my family to obey this law?" If I would not be willing to do the dirty work myself in enforcing the law, why would I think it moral to ask someone else to do it?

Using this standard, I came to the conclusion that the only moral use of government is that which I have defined in this book. I am perfectly willing to stop someone I love from committing murder, rape, enslaving another person, or stealing or vandalizing property, but not much of anything else. Most other situations I'd rather find a way to solve the problem without threatening or using violence.

I've also decided that I won't allow politicians to bribe me with favors from the public treasury. I avoid government handouts and programs as much as I can. I don't condemn people who run into hard times and are forced to rely on these programs, but I try as much as possible to avoid taking this money as I do not wish to reap the consequences of trying to get something for nothing. I prefer to labor and earn my way in this world.

Returning to the Moral Foundation of the Common Law

The common law exists regardless of the policies of government. Again, to quote Basiat:

> Life, liberty, and property do not exist because men
> have made laws. On the contrary, it was the fact that

life, liberty, and property existed beforehand that
caused men to make laws in the first place.[65]

That's why I believe that our only hope for a free society is to educate people about these moral principles and encourage them to apply
them to their own lives. To the extent that our legal system is not in
alignment with these moral principles, our society will suffer. In fact, as
the government increasingly abandons these moral principles, people
increasingly lose their respect for it. Frederick Bastiat understood this:

> When law and morality contradict each other, the cit-
> izen has the cruel alternative of either losing his moral
> sense or losing his respect for the law.[66]

Like George Washington and many others, John Adams, the
second president of the United States, knew that our system of government would not survive if we abandoned morality and religion:

> Our Constitution was made only for a moral and reli-
> gious people. It is wholly inadequate to the govern-
> ment of any other.[67]

If the majority of the people do not have a profound respect for the
individual rights of life, liberty, and property, then they will pressure
the government to trespass against those rights for their own benefit.
And, when they do so, the Law of the Harvest will cause them to lose
those rights because we cannot have a right we are unwilling to allow
for others.

---

[65] Bastiat, *The Law*, p 6

[66] *Ibid.* p 12

[67] http://www.john-adams-heritage.com/quotes/

My prayer is that this book has given you a greater insight into the moral laws we must obey if we wish to retain our freedom. We violate these moral laws at our own peril because failure to abide by them will ultimately cause us to lose our freedom, our property, and perhaps, even our lives. On the other hand, if we repent and cease to trespass against one another, God will heal our land and allow us to maintain our liberty. My prayer is that this book will help advance this cause so that the cause of freedom can ring in America for many generations to come.

Epilogue

When I was in fifth grade, my elementary school decided to try something new. They held an election for a student governor. Fifth graders were eligible to run for the office, which they would hold as a sixth-grader the following year. I decided to run.

I had a lot of ideas, which I put forth in my campaign. I had a lot of kids helping me with posters and other campaign activities. However, in spite of all my efforts, I lost the election. According to a teacher who confided in me, I had lost by one vote.

I was a geeky kind of kid with a vivid imagination, but lousy at sports. The guy who won was athletic and popular, what we might call a jock, in opposition to me, the nerd. Through subsequent experiences with student politics, it was clear to me that elections were not about the merits of the ideas people put forth; they were more like popularity contests, who had the most popular appeal.

I see this same tendency in adult politics. It isn't often the person with the best ideas is the winner. However, that's not the point of my story.

As a sixth-grader, I suggested to the kid who had won that he put out a suggestion box to collect ideas from students. He thought that was a good idea and did so. I put all the ideas I'd had when I was running (and others I came up with through the year) into the box. And that's where the story gets interesting.

Almost everything this kid did as the school governor was to implement my ideas as if they were his own. In other words, even though

I had technically lost, I still accomplished pretty much everything I wanted to do.

This lesson that you don't have to be the person in power to make a change was driven home for me when I was a senior in high school. I was the student director of our school's little closed-circuit TV studio. Under my direction, we produced a weekly student news broadcast during homeroom. The whole school watched it.

I was the one who held tryouts for our news anchors and one of the kids I selected was a junior who was a handsome guy with a real ability to talk. He became the primary face for our newscast. With the help of the other students who worked with me, I also gathered the stories, created the segments to be aired with another student, who was the technical director, and wrote the script for the anchors to read.

As a junior, my primary anchorman decided to run for next year's student body president. He won by a landslide, and he even admitted that it was because I had put him in front of the entire student body almost every week and helped him to look good. Once again, I was not the one in the front but the one behind the scenes who held the real power.

Again, you don't need to be the person in the spotlight to make a difference. If you have a desire to make a difference in our country, start right where you're at, right now. Pray and ask for guidance about how you can influence others around you in a positive way. Then, trust yourself and act. You'll ultimately win, even if it appears at first that you aren't. It's amazing how much good you can accomplish if you don't care who gets the credit. So get started making a difference today.

CPSIA information can be obtained
at www.ICGtesting.com
Printed in the USA
LVHW050719130322
713182LV00005B/13